Elizabeth Bishop and Marianne Moore

✢

Elizabeth Bishop and Marianne Moore

THE PSYCHODYNAMICS OF CREATIVITY

✝

JOANNE FEIT DIEHL

PRINCETON UNIVERSITY PRESS

PRINCETON, NEW JERSEY

Copyright © 1993 by Princeton University Press
Published by Princeton University Press, 41 William Street,
Princeton, New Jersey 08540
In the United Kingdom: Princeton University Press, Oxford
All Rights Reserved

Library of Congress Cataloging-in-Publication Data
Diehl, Joanne Feit, 1947–
Elizabeth Bishop and Marianne Moore : the psychodynamics of
creativity / Joanne Feit Diehl.
p.   cm.
Includes bibliographical references and index.
ISBN 0-691-06975-1
1. Bishop, Elizabeth, 1911–1979—Criticism and interpretation.
2. Feminism and literature—United States—History—20th century.
3. Women and literature—United States—History—20th century.
4. Moore, Marianne, 1887–1972—Criticism and interpretation.
5. American poetry—Women authors—History and criticism.   6. Women
poets, American—20th century—Psychology.   7. Modernism
(Literature)—United States.   8. Influence (Literary, artistic,
etc.)   9. Psychoanalysis and literature.   10. Authorship—Sex
differences.   11. Creative ability.   I. Title.
PS3503.I785Z634   1993   92-23533
811′.54—dc20   CIP

This book has been composed in Adobe Palatino

Princeton University Press books are
printed on acid-free paper, and meet the guidelines
for permanence and durability of the Committee
on Production Guidelines for Book Longevity
of the Council on Library Resources

Printed in the United States of America

1   3   7   9   10   8   6   4   2

FOR MY FRIENDS

✝

✣ *Contents* ✣

✥ *Acknowledgments* ✥

MY THANKS to Alan Williamson, Sandra Gilbert, and Lee Edelman for their friendship and counsel. I am grateful as well to Molly E. Daniels, the late Elliot Gilbert, and my colleagues at Bowdoin, Joseph Litvak, Steven Cerf, and Susan Bell, whose support has meant so much to me. Thanks, especially, to Cate for her continuing contribution to my understanding of mother-daughter relationships and the pleasure of her company.

Elizabeth Bishop and Marianne Moore

✣

The Muse's Monogram

Hᴀʀᴏʟᴅ Bʟᴏᴏᴍ in his *Anxiety of Influence* and Sandra Gilbert and Susan Gubar more recently in *No Man's Land* reflect upon individual authors' perceptions of the origins of their creativity and issues of intertextuality. In response to Bloom's male-identified Oedipal model of influence relations, Gilbert and Gubar posit an alternative paradigm which they label the "female affiliation complex." Arguing from a revisionist Freudian position, Gilbert and Gubar contextualize Freud's theories of female sexuality and modulate his premise of female insufficiency. Gilbert and Gubar articulate the problematic aspects of Freud's theory for women, then proceed to posit an alternative approach to questions of female literary influence, taking into account the cultural conditions under which women write and the consequent double bind for women who wish both to empower a matrilineal tradition and to keep alive the potency of their male literary inheritance. Gilbert and Gubar suggest that in order to reclaim an enabling authority for themselves, women writers may embark on a search for an adoptive foremother in a process of voyeuristic "looking at" and "looking for" an empowering literary presence. As Gilbert and Gubar write, "Given the almost vertiginous range of issues that the adoptive imperative or affiliation complex raises, looking both *at* and *for* must inevitably, again, become an essential survival strategy. For if voyeuristic looking *at* distances the woman writer from crisis even while it allows her to participate vicariously in creation, voyeuristic looking *for* enables her to validate her selected past and her elected self."[1]

Historically informed and theoretically incisive, Gilbert and Gubar's analysis remains tied to Freudian theory and the notion that "the girl's path toward maturity is far more difficult than the boy's because it is marked by imperatives of object renunciation and libidinal redirection that require enormous investments of psychic energy" (169). Gilbert and Gubar apply this developmental, psychodynamic observation to a cultural situation in which they "inevitably find women writers oscillating between their matrilineage and their patrilineage in an arduous process of self-definition" (169). To be sure, women writers experience a distinctly intense ambivalence in relation to their male and female precursors. Yet, for the purposes of theoretical clarity, I maintain that the equivalence Gilbert and Gubar assume between psychoanalysis and literary history reinscribes certain assumptions about female psychosexual development that warrant renewed investigation. Furthermore, I assert that it is only by going beyond the historically implicated Freudian model that we can reexamine the dynamics of women's relation to the literary tradition. The premise that one can "select" a literary foremother, thereby exercising an "adoptive imperative," while offering a hopeful if always difficult resolution for the vexed situation in which women writers find themselves, fails to acknowledge the psychoanalytic observation that none of us (male or female) freely *selects* any object relation, that no matter whom we choose we reenact in that new relation the interactional patterns we carry with us from our earliest past. Valuable as Gilbert and Gubar's descriptive historical analysis may be, it, therefore, does not go far enough in offering an alternative to Freudian theory.

Over against both the Bloomian and the feminist revisionary schema posited by Gilbert and Gubar, I theorize that influence relations between and among women locate their origins in the constellation of feelings best associated with Melanie Klein's description of the early feeding situation as delineated in her essay, "A Study of Envy and Gratitude" (1956). Klein's discussion of the power of the earliest infantile experiences to shape both negative and positive feelings and her interest in the impact of those feelings upon the developing psyche's conceptualization of parental figures render her work particularly potent for a consideration of the intrapsychic processes we associate with artistic production. Klein's focus upon the infantile origins of the mature individual's attitudes towards her own creativity offers a powerful heuristic model for dealing with issues related to adult creativity. Klein's emphasis upon the infant's internalization of the good and bad mother and upon the infantile anxiety that, in the process of feeding, the infant will rob the breast, that rage will destroy the mother—these concerns, in my view, can serve as a guide to an inquiry into women's literary relations. Given this interactional approach, problems surrounding gift exchange—whether the daughter will be able, without devastation to the self, to make sufficient reparation to the mother and gather sufficient supplies from the mother to produce such a gift without maternal depletion can be recognized as feelings that inform the motives and fears of the creative process. The Kleinian schema offers an insight into questions associated with the psychodynamics of creativity that both elucidates those unconscious motivations that govern a writer's production of texts and serves as a descriptive guide to the origins of the rhetorical defenses a text deploys to ward off or disguise such originatory psychic conflicts.

Klein's emphasis on the importance of envy in terms of creativeness beyond the originatory feeding situation is pertinent not only to questions of literary production in general but to influence relations in particular. Klein's assertion that "at bottom, envy is directed against creativeness: what the envied breast has to offer is unconsciously felt as the prototype of creativeness, because the breast and the milk it gives is felt to be the source of life" illuminates our understanding of the anxieties a woman writer may experience as she turns to her female literary precursor for inspiration and at the same time senses the fragility of her female predecessor's position vis-à-vis the dominant tradition of male authorship. A desire to do damage to the "mother" who is already at risk becomes yet another factor in the vexed situation of the woman writer who would align herself with an alternative female tradition because she simultaneously wishes to be endowed with the power associated with masculine-identified literary authority. How envy functions in a literary relation and how writers view their work as a form of reparation, fundamental questions that pertain to writers' conscious and unconscious assumptions about what they do (the inhibitory and empowering attitudes that influence literary production), are, therefore, enhanced by the intervention of Kleinian object-relations theory into the current debate on the psychodynamics of literary creativity.

Insofar as such a project depends upon an understanding of intertextual relationships as analogous to the transferential and countertransferential exchanges of the analysand and analyst, the underlying assumptions that govern my investigation are that there exists an authorial psyche with which other psyches interact, and that this psyche (albeit at times unbeknownst to itself) reenacts its internalized intrapsychic experience, its memories and desires, within the texts it creates. By adopting this viewpoint, one may read extra-literary and intertextual relations as parts of a single continuum that traces the trajectory of the psyche's life. If extra-literary exchanges can be referred back to the analysis of early patterns of psychosexual development, so intra- and intertextual relations can, through rhetorical interpretation, be read as encoding processes of psychic activity that find their origins in the distant, pre-Oedipal past.

My source here is a metaphor elaborated not by Melanie Klein but by her agonistic, theoretical father, Freud:

> What are transferences? They are new editions or facsimiles of the tendencies and phantasies which are aroused and made conscious during the progress of the analysis; but they have this peculiarity, which is characteristic for their species, they replace some earlier person by the person of the physician. To put it another way: a whole series of psychological experiences are revived, not as belonging to the past, but as applying to the physician at the present moment.[2]

To the extent that the analytic process can be understood as an interactive reenactment of transactions dating from early childhood, one can read such transactions as displaced narratives, stories that recount buried or repressed memories. It is but a short leap from such a narrativized understanding of analytic interaction to an interactional model for reading. If we assume that literary creativity is a psychical task, then the transference will play as great a role in the author's manipulation of words and the modelling of the fundamental instruments of literary production (his/her relation to the source of inspiration or "muse" figure, to figures of authority, to precursors, and, finally, to perceived allies and inhibitors in the creative effort) as it does in the orthodox analytic relationship per se.

In my first chapter I focus on one aspect of this complex and ongoing transferential process known as literary creativity, the poet's relation to her major precursor. The poets in question are

Elizabeth Bishop and her predecessor, the formidable Marianne Moore, whose friendship, initiated in 1934, centrally figures in the emergence of a distinctive contemporary poetics. I open this study with an examination of the general efficacy of Kleinian hermeneutics by invoking a single text, "Efforts of Affection," Bishop's posthumously published memoir of Marianne Moore on which Bishop worked sporadically over several years. I argue that Bishop's memoir contains within it a deeply ambivalent description of her relationship to her female precursor revealed through seemingly minute or merely anecdotal asides. Furthermore, this discussion opens up the interplay of the forces of envy and gratitude as they are figured throughout the memoir. Here the specific application of Kleinian theory to the Moore-Bishop relationship focuses on Bishop's portrayal of Moore to suggest how the lineaments of that portrayal are informed by the originary, oppositional tensions inherent in the Kleinian view of creativity.

The chapter that follows describes in some detail the working through of the Bishop-Moore relationship as it manifests itself in the poetry. This discussion offers intertextual readings of Moore and Bishop in order to demonstrate the ways in which Bishop builds upon her predecessor's work and how the latter poet inflects Moore's images to make them tell her own story. Characteristically, Bishop opens out Moore's closed forms to establish a subjectivity that is more tentative, provisional, and elusive than that presented by Moore. The interplay of a series of Moore and Bishop texts reveals how closely Bishop read Moore and the dramatic changes Bishop makes in the parent text as she reforms Moore's words according to her own poetic aspirations. From this sustained comparativist approach, I hope to evoke not simply the resonances of Moore in Bishop but the distinguishing swerves away from Moore that delineate Bishop's individuality. This sustained, mutual reading leads away from Moore to Bishop and concludes with a conceptualization of Bishop's poetic ethos.

The origins of that ethos inform the subject of the following chapter which examines two major works by Bishop, the poem "Crusoe in England" and the prose "In the Village," through the lens of object-relations theory. Here I draw upon Klein's "Infantile Anxiety Situations Reflected in a Work of Art and in the Creative Impulse" and, the revisionist object-relations theorist, Christopher Bollas and his work on the dream in *The Shadow of the Object*. This chapter attempts to expose the associational fabric of Bishop's poem and story to psychoanalytic theory in order to elucidate the formative, paradigmatic relationships that govern Bishop's view of the world. Bollas affords the occasion to read Bishop's poem as if it were a dream screen which recorded, through its treatment of the narrator and its disposition of the objects that surround him, a description of the poetic imagination's basic structure of relating to otherness and the roots of that structure in early infantile rejection and frustration. Klein's essay serves as the occasion for a reading of "In the Village" which again addresses the insufficient mother, this time to demonstrate a process of mourning for the wounded mother that attempts to make reparations to her. In both the poem and the story, mourning the lost mother is the primary condition against which later scenes of loss and rejection are played out. Bishop's artistic production can, I suggest, be read more generally as attempts to make reparation to the abandoning mother; through these attempts comes a process of mourning whereby Bishop seeks a compensatory gain for the lost mother or for the subsequent transferential objects that replace her. This compensatory gesture is located in masculine identification and attentiveness to the natural world, a world that is reinvested with a displaced domesticity. Loss of the mother can achieve only incomplete compensation; therefore, the yearning for the lost mother haunts these attempts at recuperation.

In the Conclusion I consider the role of object relations for elucidating the process of reading. Specifically, I speculate that an object-relations approach offers a helpful redirection of questions of literary influence. This interactional model, furthermore, enables us to investigate the processes that transpire when we read and when we write. Finally, I suggest the interpretative advantage such a gender-inflected model of poetic influence and psychodynamics offers in order to illuminate an alternative, female modernism. It is my hope that this brief volume makes a contribution to the development of a psychoanalytically informed poetics that eschews neither attention to the tropes of rhetorical figuration nor the figures of psychological form. In a future work, I plan to extend the purview of object relations beyond the focus of Bishop and Moore to consider the efficacy of applying this branch of psychoanalytic thought to the process of reading more generally. Through this preliminary reading of psychoanalysis, poetics, and aesthetic theory, I indicate the possible directions in which such an object-relations-inflected analysis can lead and the efficacy of a psychoanalytic hermeneutics for a theory of criticism.

CHAPTER ONE

"Efforts of Affection": Toward a
Theory of Female Poetic Influence

I

In "Efforts of Affection: A Memoir of Marianne Moore," Elizabeth Bishop has not only written a feelingly accurate description of Moore as friend and literary precursor, but through her delineation of that friendship more generally investigated the vexed dynamics of female literary influence. What follows is simultaneously a reading of Bishop's memoir, an interpretation of what transpires beneath the glow of approbation that characterizes Bishop's reflections on Moore, and an attempt to suggest an alternative paradigm (or at least a set of questions) that seeks to illuminate female patterns of influence. Indeed, what I will argue is that Bishop's memoir contains within it a deeply ambivalent description of her relationship to her female precursor that illuminates the psychodynamics of woman-to-woman poetic influence. Thus, my reading will attend to seemingly minute or anecdotal asides to examine the interplay of sexual identity and the psychodynamics of influence as it appears in Bishop's memoir.

From the outset, "Efforts of Affection" presents its complications in the guise of simplicity. The title itself, with its slightly old-fashioned inflection, begins the strategic process of distancing its subject while asserting a desire for intimacy. By providing an anecdotal explanation for her selection of "Efforts of Affection" as the title of the memoir, Bishop creates a complex sense of occasion, a rhetorical strategy that characterizes the memoir from its beginning to its end. Bishop recalls Moore's revision of a title in Moore's 1951 *Selected Poems*: "In my copy of this book, Marianne crossed out the 'and' and wrote 'of' above it. I liked this change very much, and so I am giving the title 'Efforts of Affection' to the whole piece" (121).[1] Although all of us recognize that love may require efforts to sustain it, Bishop's choice of the phrase as her title and her reasons for her choice suggest an insistence that draws our attention to the phrase's precise formulation. Does the phrase itself not imply a resistance to be overcome? And must the effort be repeated (hence the plural) because of a resistance within the self and/or the other that would deflect or diminish its power? Furthermore, who is making these efforts and where is their object located?

Characteristically, such questions of agency and indeterminate aggression remain unanswered as what follows masks—in order to disclose—possible answers to these questions. Furthermore, the choice of title is already implicated in questions of literary borrowing and appropriation, for by choosing "Efforts of Affection," Bishop underscores her approval of Moore's revisions of her own work.[2] The occasion for Moore's textual alteration and its significance are questions the essay does not engage. Instead, in a gesture of reciprocal appropriation, Bishop makes Moore's revision the title for her memoir. Thus, almost casually, she initiates an interrogation into the workings of intertextual exchange that becomes a dominant concern as Moore's corrective, unexplained alteration becomes Bishop's own. The terms of the essay's opening anecdote, as well as the choice of its title, direct our attention toward the psychodynamics of influence relations that emerge as the essay progresses, specifically as these relations bear on property, the inherent unknowability of the other, and the extent to which the younger poet's responses are either authenticated or censored within the determinative confines of the Moore/Bishop relationship. For, while the essay's prevailing tone is both affectionate and benign, the questions it raises suggest a much more ambivalent and contradictory scenario than one at first might surmise.

If, in the opening paragraph of "Efforts of Affection," Bishop creates her own title by borrowing a change Moore herself had made—from the coordinating conjunction "and" (which allows the words that precede and follow it to coexist) to "of" (a genitive preposition simultaneously conveying separation and origin)—Bishop returns in the memoir to the vexed question of derivation and/or conjunction in her meditations upon the phrase "manners and morals" which *she* then alters to read "manners *as* morals" only to invert the phrase to ask, "Or it is [sic] morals as manners?" (156). Her confusion once again de-

11

pends upon the status and the relationship between the two nouns, only in this case "and" is replaced by the "as" of equivalency; the question raised is whether manners, how one lives in the world, are the same as "morals," with its more explicitly ethical concern. This question remains unanswered in regard to Moore's judgment of Bishop because, throughout the memoir, Bishop, as I will demonstrate, has had to conceal her "true" self, both the fact of her mature sexuality and her sexual preference. On Moore's part, the "messages" she has sent her "daughter" add up to a condemnatory, though at times witty and feigned, censoriousness that will not allow any violation of its own proprieties at the same time that they convey an aggression and sexuality so convoluted that she simultaneously manages to assert and deny their existence. Along with the silencing of the engendered self that occurs throughout Bishop's memoir and the characterizations bordering on caricature that dominate this apparently unjudgmental, richly anecdotal description of Moore, "Efforts of Affection" presents a sustained discourse of the maternal, which bears scrutiny both for what it reveals regarding Bishop's thoughts on Moore as literary mother and for its description of the origins of the engendered aspects of influence relations more generally. For a discussion of "Efforts of Affection" in relation to psychoanalytic theory, I rely upon a work that Bishop herself recommended to Robert Lowell, a "grim little book by Melanie Klein, 'Gratitude and Envy' [sic]—superb in its horrid way."[3] What might strike one as "grim" in Klein's brilliant and dense analysis is its tendency toward biological essentialism, its ascription of such enormous importance to the first months of life, and the determinative effects of the mother-infant relationship over which the mother herself exercises almost no conscious control. Grim, too, perhaps, is Klein's characterization of the infant as possessing, for its own survival, those qualities that psychoanalysis identifies in the adult as "pathological." The "depressive," "paranoid," and "schizophrenic" positions become (in Kleinian theory) the means by which the infant survives in her/his world. Although the use of these ordinarily "pathological" terms might also initially appear "grim," Klein's deployment of them enables the reader to look beyond the stigmatization of psychoanalytic naming to observe the potentially melioristic functions of the psychic phenomena themselves.

Reading Klein in the context of literary influence relations, one notes the degree to which the infant's relationship to the maternal, specifically and emblematically to the mother's breast, determines the child's, and later the adult's, experience of the world.[4] If all relationships (including those of reading) are inherently transferential, if reading and living as acts of interpretation are informed by our earliest "object relations," then one might examine Bishop's relationship to Moore as an outgrowth of Bishop's earliest relationship with her own mother. Immediately, critical difficulties multiply, for what we possess constitutes only the vaguest surmise—a mother who experiences a series of "breakdowns" and is institutionalized when Bishop is five years old, a relationship so painful as to express itself aesthetically, in the poems, in the image of the dry or hard breast, or by the erasure of the mother through dis-engenderment or silence.[5] Given Bishop's deeply controlled and disciplined poetics, it might be heuristically advantageous to read the apparently casual "Efforts of Affection" in a distinctly antithetical context, as the encoded story of Bishop's primal relationship and its subsequent literary reenactment. Such a reading of "Efforts of Affection" reveals a paradigm of maternal influence that could transferentially be extended to any sublimating activity, either the art of reading or literary friendship itself. That Bishop, at the memoir's close, sees in Moore's monogram the word "mother" leads to an even more direct association; the mother one discovers, as I will suggest, is confusing, censorious, and willful, at the same time that she masks these negative qualities by a decorum and extraordinary linguistic playfulness that her poetic daughter not only admires but wishes to appropriate.

From Bishop's cumulative descriptions, Moore emerges as a powerful literary mother, controlling and manipulative as well as terrifyingly unique. At the same time, Bishop's portrait of Moore attempts to accommodate the censoring presence of the literary mother while drawing attention to her prudery, unworldliness, and refusal to engage in the complexities of the human unconscious or to confront the issue of sexuality itself.[6] Whatever the individual occasion, Bishop's memoir strives to

13

come to terms with the presence of aggression and its implications for a woman poet in her dealings with her most forbidding and immediate literary precursor. How to evade Moore's censoriousness, how to remain "loyal" yet simultaneously to contain her precursor's power by delineating her "weaknesses" or idiosyncracies is the central problem "Efforts of Affection" confronts and fails to resolve.

Granted that Bishop's admiration and respect for Moore remain powerful motivations throughout the memoir, it is out of this very affection that the conflicts themselves arise. Bishop's literary knowledge of Moore preceded their first meeting, and the story of the meeting itself, with its astonishing details, continues to construct a site of conflict, affection, and danger. What Bishop describes when she recalls first reading Moore's work is the experience of a young poet discovering in her precursor the redefinition of poetry itself.

> I hadn't known poetry could be like that; I took to it immediately, but although I knew there was a volume of hers called *Observations*, it was not in the library and I had never seen it. (121)

This assessment of the immediate impact of Moore's work upon Bishop, as well as the difficulty of actually finding her poems, leads to a digression that nevertheless centers upon what the essay subsequently will clarify. Bishop offers the following explanation for the digression: "Because Miss Borden [the Vassar college librarian] seems like such an appropriate person to have introduced me to Marianne Moore, I want to say a little about her" (121). But that little is extremely intriguing, for while the obvious effect of the description of the subdued, intensely shy librarian, Miss Fanny Borden, meshes with the shyness and reserve Bishop will later associate with Moore herself, the librarian is important in other ways as well. For, Miss Borden, as Bishop recalls, "was the niece of the Fall River Lizzie Borden, and at college the rumor was that Lizzie Borden's lurid career had had a permanently subduing effect on Miss Fanny Borden's personality. She was extremely shy and reserved and spoke in such a soft voice it was hard to hear her at all. (She was tall and thin; she always dressed in brown and grays, old-fashioned, muted, and distinguished-looking.)" (121–122). In her description of the reserved Miss Borden, not only does Bishop provide a reason for the librarian's manner, but she also brings into her narrative the figure of Lizzie Borden herself, accused and later acquitted of the ax murder of her elderly mother and father in Falls River, New York. The allusion to daughterly violence remains in the shadows as a background that, however silently, gestures toward the aggression so carefully controlled throughout the text, an historical reference that contributes to the memoir's rather disquieting tone. All apparent affection, the essay is laced with an aggression confined within the brackets of anecdote and verbal aside.

The Vassar Miss Borden, so unlike the woman who shares her name, rides a chainless bicycle, and Bishop's description of this procedure contains something of the sense of performance that will later characterize her understanding of Moore's poetic singularity. "I remember," Bishop writes, "watching her ride slowly up to the library, seated very high and straight on this curiosity, which somehow seemed more lady-like than a bicycle with a chain, and park it in the rack. (We didn't padlock bicycles then.)" (122). The importance of defining what is "ladylike" and what is not will remain a concern throughout the memoir but is here associated with oddity and the impossibility of duplication. The combination of dignity and the appearance of curiosity (later aligned with the grotesque) characterize Bishop's subsequent descriptions of Moore, wherein helplessness and condescension mark Bishop's reactions to her predecessor's evident singularity. The parenthetical "we didn't padlock bicycles then," moreover, conveys the sense of a bygone time when trust could be assumed. Possession, appropriation, and violation of trust, subjects that will later reappear in a literary context, are thus first introduced in regard to a simple but indecipherable object. Intrigued, Bishop recalls that "once, after she had gone inside, I examined the bicycle, which was indeed chainless, to see if I could figure out how it worked. I couldn't" (122). The mystery of the bicycle's mechanism proliferates throughout the memoir as Bishop insists upon Moore's originality and the impossibility of penetrating its origins.

Not only is Miss Fanny Borden, the purveyor of Moore's volume, surrounded by an aura of mystery and hidden violence, but the scene of Bishop's borrowing Moore's book is itself profoundly evocative:

15

> Contact with the librarian was rare; once in a long while, in search
> of a book, one would be sent into Miss Borden's office, shadowy
> and cave-like, with books piled everywhere. She weighed down
> the papers on her desk with smooth, round stones, quite big
> stones, brought from the seashore, and once when my roommate
> admired one of these, Miss Borden said in her almost inaudible
> voice, 'Do you like it? You may *have* it,' and handed it over, gray,
> round, and very heavy. (122)

Her shadowy cave-like office resembles the home of an ancient
oracle, and the books, papers, and smooth, round stones
brought from the seashore create an interior in which texts
stand alongside natural objects, for this is a cave in which books
inform the scenery of life. (One recalls the liminal landscape of
"The Sea and Its Shore," where the difference between texts and
natural objects similarly disappears.) Within this oracular, cave-
like office, the librarian gives a gift, gives it in a way that recalls
the final moment in Bishop's poem "The Man-Moth," when the
bestowal of a gift depends upon a reciprocal act of attention. On
a purely verbal level as well, the description of the librarian's
gift echoes the closing lines of Bishop's poem:

> . . . Then from the lids
> One tear, his only possession, like the bee's sting, slips.
> Slyly he palms it, and if you're not paying attention
> he'll swallow it. However, if you watch, he'll hand it over,
> cool as from underground springs and pure enough to drink.

"Hand[ed] it over" followed by the description of the object
(stone or tear) combined with a sense of effortfulness link the
two moments. Concerning the value of Marianne Moore's poetry, however, the librarian has her doubts, for she responds
with a certain skepticism when Bishop asks why the Vassar College library has no copies of Moore. "Do you *like* Marianne
Moore's poems?" she asked (122). This question, so closely
modelled upon the question Miss Borden had just asked about
the rock, "Do you like it?," conveys in its negative emphasis her
difference of tone.

Once in possession of the dubious book, Bishop records her
own impressions:

> Miss Borden's copy of *Observations* was an eye-opener in more
> ways than one. Poems like 'An Octopus,' about a glacier, or

'Peter,' about a cat, or 'Marriage,' about marriage, struck me, as they still do, as miracles of language and construction. Why had no one ever written about things in this clear and dazzling way before? (123)

Although her response ends with "clear" and "dazzling" praise, the preceding sentence, with its overtly reductive simplifications—its reiterative naming—suggests a mocking insouciance, as does the more generalized characterization of these poems as "miracles of language and construction," a phrase that recalls Bishop's "Invitation to Miss Marianne Moore":

> With dynasties of negative constructions
> darkening and dying around you,
> with grammar that suddenly turns and shines
> like flocks of sandpipers flying,
>   please come flying.

Completed after "Invitation to Miss Marianne Moore," "Efforts of Affection" shares this poem's deeply ambivalent vision.[7]

The specific conditions Moore demands for their first meeting serve both as a protection for the older woman and a trial for the younger. Earlier meetings with other interested Vassar girls had proven failures, a fact that Bishop was only later to learn. The conditions for, as Bishop terms it, their "first rendezvous" were that she "was to find Miss Moore seated on the bench at the right of the door leading to the reading room of the New York Public Library" (123–124). These instructions are immediately followed by the statement that the terms "might have been even more strict." Bishop "learned later that other would-be acquaintances" Moore "really expected *not* to like, she arranged to meet . . . at the Information Booth in Grand Central Station—no place to sit down, and, if necessary, an instant getaway was possible" (123–124). Such deliberate efforts to control occasions suggest the need for camouflage, the nervousness of a skittish and furtive creature poised for escape. Miss Borden's description of Moore reaffirms her fey and childlike furtiveness:

> a strange and appealing little creature with bright red hair—playful, and, as might have been expected, fond of calling her family and friends by the names of animals. (124)

Yet this description does little to calm Bishop's fears on her first trip to meet Moore: "I was very frightened," she writes, "but I put on my new spring suit and took the train to New York" (124). Although Bishop's vision of Moore remains one of intimidating authority, the sequence of passages, the first presenting Moore as a child and the second describing Bishop as a frightened young woman, serves to bridge the generational difference with mutual fear. In what passes for simple temporal description, Bishop once again suggests the dialectics of anteriority:

> I was right on time, even a bit early, but she was there before me (no matter how early one arrived, Marianne was always there first) and, I saw at once, not very tall and not in the least intimidating. (124)

Always to find the other there first no matter how early one arrives is surely to experience the burden of literary as well as personal belatedness. One recalls, in this regard, Emerson's lament that wherever he goes he finds Plato coming back. The need always to be there and waiting can itself be read as a sign of aggression on the older woman's part, a punctiliousness that functions as a guard against surprise, or against *being taken by surprise*. It is, as so many of the gestures that Bishop associates with Moore indicate, a bid for mastery over time and the "other," an attempt to control.

In terms of the "Family Romance," what emerges as early as Bishop's and Moore's first meeting and develops over time is a quasi mother-daughter relationship in which the "daughter" expresses, although she does not always overtly acknowledge, deeply ambivalent feelings regarding a powerful, dangerously manipulative "mother" who has a strong desire to control her actions as well as to insist upon her own unremitting affection. Presented as completely "original," Moore is inherently defined as apart from the poetic tradition (or, for that matter, from other women), an oddity, an outcast, who lives in a domestic sanctuary of the antique, and whose confrontations with contemporary culture are characterized by an uncanny ability to disarm various forms of masculine aggression. Such a characterization enables Bishop to inscribe a crucial difference between herself and her inimitable literary mother, for Bishop navigates in the contemporary with an assurance and knowledge that dates and circumscribes Moore's experience all the more. In her modernity, her worldliness, and her openness to

experience, Bishop distinguishes herself from Moore's controlling, restrictive attitude toward all that surrounds her. Note
specifically how, in regard to dress, Bishop attempts to antique
her:

> The large flat black hat was as I'd expected it to be. She wore a
> blue tweed suit that day and, as she usually did then, a man's
> 'polo shirt,' as they were called, with a black bow at the neck. The
> effect was quaint, vaguely Bryn Mawr 1909, but stylish at the
> same time. I sat down and she began to talk. (124)

Bishop's ambivalence even shades what she appears to most
value. Describing their first encounter, Bishop continues, "It
seems to me that Marianne talked to me steadily for the next
thirty-five years, but of course that is nonsensical" (124). Nonsensical though it might be, the illusion abides. In admiring the
brilliance of Moore's conversation, Bishop again stresses its absolute uniqueness: "She must have been one of the world's
greatest talkers: entertaining, enlightening, fascinating, and
memorable; her talk, like her poetry, was quite different from
anyone else's in the world" (124). And yet it was, at least after
their initial meeting, entirely forgettable. "I don't know what
she talked about at that first meeting; I wish I had kept a diary"
(124). Although it is difficult to assess the function of this forget-
fulness, it certainly questions the "memorability" that Bishop
has just chosen to praise.

   With the serendipity that often marks the course of true
friendship, Bishop invites Moore to the circus. Although Bishop
takes Moore's acceptance of her invitation as a personal tri-
umph, in actuality Moore made such a visit an annual event.
As with the history of Vassar girls whom Moore had disliked,
ignorance of the more threatening reality, or in this case a reality
that attributes less significance to Bishop's power to secure a
friendship, protects her from what might otherwise have been
a deeper insecurity. That Bishop subsequently discloses the
"truth" about her earlier ignorance of these occasions (Moore's
disappointment with other Vassar girls and her having planned
to attend the circus anyway) creates a readerly awareness of the
lapse of time and identity between the naive narrative "self"
and her present "self," worldly and perhaps only now fully ap-
prised of a somewhat more threatening reality vis-à-vis her rela-

tion to Moore. Bishop reflects on her prior innocence as, with the wisdom of age, she writes:

> I didn't know that she *always* went to the circus, wouldn't have missed it for anything, and when she accepted, I went back to Poughkeepsie in the grimy day coach extremely happy. (125)

Thus, the youthful illusion of happiness is taken away at the very moment that it is expressed.

The "circus" recollection, while full of humor and recollected pleasure, as well as evidence of Bishop's acknowledgment of Moore's nurturance, protectiveness, and passionate curiosity, contains elements that suggest a more ambivalent story. Bishop arrives on the scene early, and once again "Marianne was there ahead of" her (125). Bishop discovers, moreover, that Moore has a plan in which Bishop will serve as a necessary accomplice. In order to replace strands missing from her elephant-hair bracelet, Moore wants to clip a few hairs from a baby elephant's tuft, while Bishop will distract the animal with the stale brown bread Moore has brought along for the occasion. This is, of course, amusing and renders Moore, in her eccentricity, at once distinctly peculiar and real. Yet humor rather than silencing permits the aggression of Moore's gesture to slip by almost unnoticed. Moore triumphs; she gets the elephant hairs; but the need to appropriate, to take something from an animal to replace what she herself has lost, and her use of Bishop to complete the act, suggests a kind of violation as well.

Distancing herself from Moore, Bishop notes, "I hate seeing animals in cages, especially small cages, and especially circus animals, but I think that Marianne, while probably feeling the same way, was so passionately interested in them, and knew so much about them, that she could put aside any pain or outrage for the time being" (126). Bishop here is making a moral distinction—to be able to put aside pain or outrage for the sake of a passionate interest bespeaks a desire for appropriation that involves a disregard for others. But Moore, according to Bishop, also has an intimate acquaintance with the natural that may be, or at least appears to be, mutual. When Moore and Bishop observe a snake writhing about in a glass-walled cage, seeming deliberately to raise his head to look at them, Moore exclaims,

20

"See, he knows me! He remembers me from last year." Bishop comments, "This was a joke, I decided, but perhaps not altogether a joke." Just how far Moore's power extends, whether it indeed embraces such extraordinary possibilities, remains a question that when later applied to poetry acquires a troubling significance. Moore has taken along food for her and her guest, orange juice, hard-boiled eggs (the yolks only), and more brown bread, "but fresh this time, and buttered" (126). Not only does she provide for herself and her guest, but Moore is attentive (almost obtrusively so) to the needs of others. Seated behind a father and his children at the circus, Moore offers her assistance:

> A big circus goes for a long time and the children began to grow restless. Marianne leaned over with the abruptness that characterized all her movements and said to the father that if the little girl wanted to go to the bathroom, she'd be glad to take her. (126)

Here as elsewhere Moore asserts her presence in gestures of apparent benevolence but also with a slight quality of meddlesomeness. Ever thoughtful, Moore's concern itself becomes, by the close of the essay, an occasion for anxiety. The need to control, to care for others when such solicitude is *not* requested, re-emerges when Moore keeps reminding the adult Bishop to go to the bathroom or to take a nickel for the subway ride home. In terms of familial psychology, these are the "good mother's" standard, hidden weapons that breed her child's growing resentment. How could anyone resent someone so thoughtful? How could anyone not?

When Bishop visits the Moores (Marianne and her mother), the issue of priority, of overcoming Moore's oppressive thoughtfulness, again invests the most minute and ordinary occasions with a sense of competition and consequent anxiety. Here is Bishop taking (or trying to take) the elevator:

> The elevator was small and slow. After I had buzzed, I used to try to get up in it to the fourth floor before Marianne could get down in it to take me up personally, but I rarely managed to. (127)

Such control makes the achievement of independence border on the impossible. Similarly, the Moores' injunction that guests take a nickel from the "famous bowl of nickels for subway fare":

21

Every visitor was made to accept one of these upon leaving; it was absolutely *de rigueur*. After one or two attempts at refusing, I always simply helped myself to a nickel as I left, and eventually I was rewarded for this by Marianne's saying to a friend who was protesting, 'Elizabeth is an *aristocrat*; she *takes* the money. (127)

Elizabeth's "aristocracy" depends upon her reassertion of authority, converting obligation into a matter of willed choice, a strategy Bishop employs throughout her relationship with Moore in order to preserve her autonomy. Even her name is subjected to Moore's appropriative sensibility, as she pronounces "Elizabeth" with an idiosyncratic emphasis on the second syllable, a change Bishop notes with approval:

She came down very hard on the second syllable, El*iz*abeth. I liked this, especially as an exclamation, when she was pretending to be shocked by something I had said. (127)

The playfulness of this interaction is based upon a double-gamesmanship in which each partner parries a verbal thrust in good-natured defiance. Moore mispronounces Bishop's name in response to the provocation of Bishop's saying something that only apparently shocks her, a deception of which Bishop, cast as rebellious, worldly younger woman, is herself aware. The recognition that she has only apparently shocked Moore pleases Bishop, and the result is a silent communication of mutual understanding in which a feigned offence is met by a deliberate, although hardly injurious violation. It is the playfulness of intimacy, a way of deflecting aggression through humor—a tactic both poets, in their work, deploy with masterly accuracy.

II

. . . modestly vain of her manual skills. A set of carpenter's tools hung by the kitchen door. . . . In one doorway a "trapeze on chains" was looped up to the lintel . . . and she said that when she exercised on it and her brother was there, he always said, "The ape is rattling her chains again!" A chest stood in the bay window of the living room with a bronze head of Marianne on it by Lachaise. The chest was also always piled high with new books.

> When I first knew Marianne she did quite a bit of reviewing and
> later sold the review copies on West Fourth Street. (128)

The portrait of the woman in her surroundings is at once eccen-
tric, particular, and contradictory. Strength, elegance, and prag-
matism are the qualities Bishop ostensibly admires in Moore.
Furthermore, when Bishop enters the Moore house, she suc-
cumbs to its manners, trying to smoke only one or two ciga-
rettes, "or none at all" because she felt Mrs. Moore "disapproved," and when occasionally "given a glass of Dubonnet to
drink," Bishop suspects the bottle is kept for her pleasure alone.
The elder Mrs. Moore surveys this censorious atmosphere with
irony and devotion. "Her manner toward Marianne was that of
a kindly, self-controlled parent who felt that she had to take a
firm line, that her daughter might be given to flightiness or—
an equal sin, in her eyes—mistakes in grammar" (129). Parental style affects language and behavior equally. Bishop, moreover, notes how maternal presence influences Moore's literary
style, for Mrs. Moore is described as being clearly instrumental
in determining both the subjects and the language of Moore's
poems.

> Waiting for the conclusion of her longer statements, I grew rather
> nervous; nevertheless, I found her extreme precision enviable and
> thought I could detect echoes of Marianne's own style in it: the
> use of double or triple negatives, the lighter and wittier ironies—
> Mrs. Moore had provided a sort of ground bass for them. (129)

Moore's mother, a devout woman, tries to impose her own religious views on Bishop. "She said grace before dinner, and once,
a little maliciously, I think Marianne asked *me* to say grace. Mercifully, a childhood grace popped into my mind" (129). Again
the slightly mischievous cast of "Marianne's" humor appears,
and once again, Bishop dutifully obeys, this time the secular dis-
believer retrieving from childhood memory the requisite grace,
as "mercifully," with its echoes of a world in which God could
bestow his love, is translated into a secular and subordinate ad-
verb. But Marianne is implicated in this occasion as well, for
"after dinner [she] wrote it down." Once again Bishop describes
without commentary; how are we to interpret this "writing
down"—as a gesture of appropriation, as a desire to record?

Surely, the censorious, religious atmosphere of the Moore household informs Bishop's attitudes toward the older poet's limitations and to the restrictive quality of her life. In this regard, Bishop consistently, albeit discreetly, challenges the norms of sexual convention in order to restore to the rather flat account of Moore's "over-fastidiousness" its potential impact upon her own sense of difference. Sexual mores are equated with religious righteousness in a way that would certainly have caused Bishop to hide her own sexual proclivities and to remain silent regarding the freedom of her sexual choices. She writes:

> I remember her [Moore's] worrying about the fate of a mutual friend whose sexual tastes had always seemed quite obvious to me: "What are we going to do about X...? Why, sometimes I think he may even be in the clutches of a *sodomite*...!" One could almost smell the brimstone. (130)

Novels of the "thirties and the forties . . . were taken down to the cellar and burned in the furnace," and Bishop is reprimanded for having used the word "spit." She is scolded, too, for having used "water closet" in her poem "Roosters," but "by then [she] had turned obstinate" (130). The complexities of Moore's evasions of the sexual aspects of contemporary society, her "over-fastidiousness," as Bishop prefers to call it, and Moore's sense of propriety become questions of literary and contextual style. Rules, especially self-created rules, are to be followed as devotion to form governs all personal and artistic endeavor.

Yet there is, of course, a sharp narrative disjunction between the notions of propriety established by the Moore ménage and the memoir that depicts them. Discussing the importance of clothes and costume, Bishop describes the Moores "making over" a pair of Marianne Moore's "drawers" and then moves on to the more general category of underwear. A sense of trespass accompanies Bishop's transcriptions of these details of domestic life even as one is charmed by them. "Several times over the years Marianne asked me abruptly, 'Elizabeth what do you have on under your dress? How much underwear do you wear?'" Moore's question, in its explicitly practical and curiously straightforward unself-consciousness, denies all hints at prurience, and the contrast between Bishop's enumeration of her "two or perhaps three undergarments," and Moore's manifold layers again suggests the difference between the antiquated Moore and the modern, stripped-down Bishop (133). Indeed, the subject of clothing itself becomes charged with the recurrent issue of control, when, for example, Moore responds with shock to Bishop's conforming to contemporary custom:

> And sometimes when I arrived on a cold winter evening dressed in a conventional way, I would be greeted by 'Elizabeth, silk stockings!' as if I were reckless or prone to suicide. My own clothes were subject to her careful consideration. (133)

The vehemence of Moore's response, as Bishop tells it, is out of all keeping with the risks of apparel. Yet the question is once again that of Moore's unrelenting sense of propriety, a propriety tantamount to a prescriptive code of manners and its inextricable relationship to a view of life so restrictive as to interpret any deviance as equivalent to madness or to sin.

As in her description of Moore's apartment where three disjunct images converge, Bishop constructs her paragraph on Moore's physical appearance by breaching decorum to intermix literary, sexual, and creaturely associations, thereby creating an insouciant portrait of the charmingly grotesque. First Moore is envisioned as the wild jungle girl Rima in W. H. Hudson's *Green Mansions* (one recalls Bishop's earlier allusion to the trapeze), as Moore's eyes remind Bishop "of a small animal, that often looked at one sidewise—quickly, at the conclusion of a sentence that had turned out unusually well, to see if it had taken effect." This description of furtiveness, desire for approval, and need to register the effect of one's otherwise covert wit is followed by an even more provocative image:

> Her face was small and pointed, but not really triangular because it was a little lopsided, with a delicately pugnacious-looking jaw. When one day I told her she looked like Mickey Rooney, then a very young actor (and she did), she seemed quite pleased. (133)

The pugnacity, though delicate, is nevertheless present and contributes to an audacious description which at once views Moore as a passionate, romantic heroine, a furtive small animal, and a brash, young, male actor, a wonderfully apt portrait that defies categorizations of gender and surely all conventional notions of narrative propriety as well.[8]

25

Continuing in its associational recollections, the memoir describes Moore's laugh, which contains within it a complexity of feeling that denies as it revels in another's right to praise her. How one accepts compliments is, of course, a good clue to larger issues of personality, and Moore's mode of amused deflection conjoins a certain disparagement with real pleasure:

> She accepted compliments with this laugh too, without words; it disparaged and made light of them, and implied that she and her audience were both far above such absurdities. I believe she was the only person I have ever known who "bridled" at praise, while turning pink with pleasure. These gestures of her head were more pronounced in the presence of gentlemen because Marianne was innately flirtatious. (134)

To bridle at praise while turning pink with pleasure is to enact the conflictual feelings associated with rendering oneself vulnerable to another's opinion, and the consequence of such a response is to convert that "other" into an "audience" (134).

Similarly, and on a grander scale, the exchange of gifts becomes an activity fraught with difficulty for the giver, again apparently because of the implicit, unstated standards that Moore revealed only after the gift itself had been received. The fear, when giving Moore a gift, was always that it would be taken as a "burden." Such a bid for power, for control over everything that can be done to or for the self, diminishes the ability of the other to act and forces her/him into a position of tentativeness, insecurity, and doubt.

> One never knew what would succeed, but one learned that if a gift did not succeed it would be given back, unobtrusively, but somehow or other, a year or two later. My most successful gift was a pair of gloves. (134)

The silent reproof of tact, Moore's return of an unsuccessful gift, is certainly consistent with the censorious, judgmental image of Moore that Bishop has already created. Always to arrive first, to direct another adult to use the bathroom, to be scandalized by a difference in dress, to evaluate gifts upon an undefined standard that can only be guessed at by the giver— these are mechanisms of control that if present in the mother or in the transferential literary mother, create obstacles in the daughter's struggle for autonomy and for her affirmation of independence.

Regarding explicitly literary matters, Bishop's other "very successful" gift to Moore is "a paper nautilus" that becomes the subject of Moore's poem of that name. Bishop quotes Moore's lines in "Efforts of Affection":

> ... its wasp-nest flaws
> of white on white, and close-

> laid Ionic chiton-folds
> like the lines in the mane of
> a Parthenon horse ...

Interestingly, in her poem, "Santarém," Bishop may be observed subtly taking back or provisionally reappropriating her gift, although she does not allude to the possibility of this reappropriation in the memoir itself. The lines from Bishop's poem are themselves related to the subject of gift exchange, the rejection of someone else's attribution of value to an object, the utterly uncomprehending sensibility of one who cannot recognize the value of what the poem's speaker had so genuinely admired that the owner made it a gift:

> In the blue pharmacy the pharmacist
> had hung an empty wasps' nest from a shelf:
> small, exquisite, clean matte white,
> and hard as stucco. I admired it
> so much he gave it to me.
> Then—my ship's whistle blew. I couldn't stay.
> Back on board, a fellow-passenger, Mr. Swan,
> Dutch, the retiring head of Philips Electric,
> really a very nice old man,
> who wanted to see the Amazon before he died,
> asked, "What's that ugly thing?"[9]

In its transposition from Moore's paper nautilus to Bishop's wasp nest, the image has shed its flaws, becoming "exquisite," "clean matte white." In Moore's poem, the paper nautilus is an object too precious

> For authorities whose hopes
> are shaped by mercenaries?
> Writers entrapped by
> teatime fame and by
> commuters' comforts? ...[10]

The gift is self-made, constructed by the sea-creature for her eggs, which free her from confinement only when they themselves are freed. Thus, Moore's poem engages issues of gift-exchange and the interdependence of the maternal and her offspring. Yet this reciprocity is fraught with difficulty, as well as the need to guard what cannot easily be spared. In both poems, moreover, the object's value is judged superior to conventional powers of appreciation. When, in Moore's poem, "the paper nautilus / constructs her thin glass shell," she creates a "perishable / souvenir of hope" that demands a "watchful maker" who "guards it / day and night." "Buried eight-fold in her eight / arms," she is compared to Hercules, the hero who must labor, but her labor is explicitly associated with the maternal, for only when the eggs leave the shell is the paper nautilus released: "the intensively / watched eggs coming from / the shell free it when they are freed." The poem's choice of subject, its description of labor, birth, and the mutual bond between the maternal and its offspring, are silently echoed in Bishop's allusion to Moore's poem, explicated only by the memoir's associational freedoms.

A deadly coral snake Bishop gives Moore is, however, not such a success, yet no words are exchanged on the subject until years later: "A mutual friend told me that Marianne was relieved; she had always hated it." The apparent capriciousness of Moore's taste (her aversion to red and then her praise of a red padlock on her favorite piece of luggage) again renders Moore completely unpredictable, if not totally baffling.[11] Such bafflement, with its element of mystery, most strongly resembles a child's failure to comprehend the rules that govern an adult's discrete choices. With Moore, the reader learns, as adult or as child, one never knew quite where one stood.

Bishop characterizes the "atmosphere of 260 Cumberland Street" (a place encumbered by rules and rituals) as "old-fashioned, but even more, otherworldly—as if one were living in a diving bell from a different world, let down through the crass atmosphere of the twentieth century" (137). What, one wonders, were the consequences for Bishop and for Moore of such otherworldliness? Like the man-moth who travels among strangers and always travels backwards, when Bishop leaves the "diving bell" to ride back to Manhattan, she finds it difficult to reconcile the Moores' world with all that lies beyond it: the "stories, phrases, the unaccustomed deference, the exquisitely prolonged etiquette—these were hard to reconcile with the New Lots Avenue express and the awful, jolting ride facing a row of indifferent faces" (137). Initially, however, Bishop describes the effect of her visits as morally uplifting:

> Yet I never left Cumberland Street without feeling happier: uplifted, even inspired, determined to be good, to work harder, not to worry about what other people thought, never to try to publish anything until I thought I'd done my best with it, no matter how many years it took—or never to publish at all. (137)

The determination to work harder, to free oneself of others' judgment, ends, however, with the thought that perhaps Moore's standards were so high one should "never publish at all."

Indeed, Moore's own perfectionism could be daunting and, the obsessiveness that went along with it, destructive. Bishop comments on all the effort that was lost when in the *Collected Poems* (1951), Moore "had already begun a ruthless cutting of some of her most beautiful poems, and what suffered chiefly from this ruthlessness were those very rhymes and stanza forms she had so painstakingly elaborated in the years just before" (139). In order to begin to come to terms with Moore as a poet, with her perfectionism as well as her power, Bishop, for her own "amusement," develops a myth of originality, of the absolute uniqueness that dominates all aspects of Moore's life and work:

> She looked like no one else; she talked like no one else; her poems showed a mind not much like anyone else's; and her notions of meter and rhyme were unlike all the conventional notions—so why not believe that the old English meters that still seem natural to most of us (or *seemed* to, at any rate) were not natural to her at all? That Marianne from birth, physically, had been set going to a different rhythm? Or was the explanation simply that she had a more sensitive ear than most of us, and since she had started writing at a time when poetry was undergoing drastic changes, she had been free to make the most of it and experiment as she saw fit? (139–140)

Both explanations, the playful biological one and the appeal to a singular historical set of circumstances, fend off the possibility of duplication—either you are Marianne Moore or you are not.

Yet this uniqueness does not simplify the vexed ethics of literary borrowing. When Bishop supplies Moore with what to her is a self-evident rhyme, Moore responds, "Elizabeth, thank you, you have saved my life!" If the wearing of silk stockings on a cold night could signify that one were reckless or prone to suicide, a rhyme might very well proffer salvation. Interestingly, such hyperbole co-exists alongside a rigid decorum that apparently governs all except the most intimate or the most staged of relationships. Bishop's contributions to Moore's translations of La Fontaine, and Moore's gratitude, teach Bishop (as if she needed to learn) the isolation of individuality and the exclusive loneliness that such originality inevitably entails:

> But they made me realize more than I ever had the rarity of true originality, and also the sort of alienation it might involve. (140)

Not only does this observation implicitly distinguish Moore from Bishop, but it also enables Bishop to identify with those others, to deny the very singularity that she herself possessed.

The issue of literary borrowing is of course a difficult one for all writers, but especially noteworthy in Bishop's description is her assertion of Moore's scrupulosity followed by her confession that she does have "one very slight grudge." While admiring Moore for her exceptionally rigorous honesty, an honesty that borders on literal-mindedness, Bishop nevertheless notes that Moore borrowed a phrase from Bishop, a phrase that refers to glass buoy-balls carried by "a very old porter": "The bellboy with the buoy-balls." Liking "the sound of this," Bishop repeats "the phrase to Marianne a day or so later," and it reappears without a note in the fifth stanza of "Four Quartz Crystal Clocks." Bishop cannot reconcile this with what she had come to expect of Moore. "It was so thoroughly out of character for her to do this that I have never understood it," she confesses (141). The obvious sexual reference, moreover, cannot help but complicate matters, for, if Bishop is aware of it, she gives no sign that either she or Moore recognizes the double entendre. That Moore should have used the phrase without herself being aware of the pun seems odd, but perhaps Bishop's including the incident is her way of quietly getting back at the prudish, unworldly Moore who has used her phrase but has not understood it. Self-conscious about her own resentment, Bishop reflects, "I am sometimes appalled to think how much I may have unconsciously stolen from her. Perhaps we are all magpies" (141). With the apparent randomness of associational recollection that characterizes the memoir, Bishop next considers the subject of silence, and although she alludes to silence as simply "another one of Marianne's convictions," her discussion of reticence and Moore's hesitation regarding dedications of literary works certainly speaks as a silent tribute to the debt Bishop must have realized she owed Moore. As Bishop describes Moore's literary world and how she manoeuvers in it, she refers to two occasions that, albeit obliquely, convey Moore's sense of herself in relation to literary tradition, particularly in regard to the issues of gender posed by the tradition itself.

Initially, the subject of dedication provides the link between Bishop's discussions of literary borrowing and Moore's literary milieu. The dedication Bishop cites is Marianne Moore's to her mother, a dedication that directly engages both the themes of the maternal and the fear of inadequacy. Bishop cites it in full:

> "Dedications imply giving, and we do not care to make a gift of what is insufficient; but in my immediate family there is one 'who thinks in a particular way' and I should like to add that where there is an effect of thought or pith in these pages, the thinking and often the actual phrases are hers."(142)

Despite the formality of its locution, one cannot imagine a more intimate example of the conflation of literary and personal indebtedness. When one assesses Mrs. Moore's contributions to her daughter's work, as Bishop presents them, they are associated with a propriety of diction and an attention to form that pervade the Moores' fastidious approach to both life and language.

Outside the biological family, Moore's sense of literary competition was apparently fairly intense, resulting in a combative verbal strategy reminiscent of the rhetorical defensiveness of the poems (a subject to which I return in the next chapter). On a number of occasions, Moore deflects the issue of literary or personal evaluation by meticulously and humorously commenting upon appearance or the details of personal style. If she treats her contemporaries with the armor of wit, she responds to Bishop's mentioning Walt Whitman with mock horror. "Elizabeth, don't speak to me about that man!" Bishop notes, "So I never did again." Bishop's submissive obedience and Moore's mock-ferocious sense of outrage affirm Bishop's difference and her compliance, the degree to which, at least in Moore's presence, she was willing to defer to her predecessor's notions of propriety and of values even when they might be putatively feigned.

When Moore is attacked by feminists, "one of whom described her as a 'poet who controlled panic by presenting it as whimsy,' " Bishop closes ranks: "Whimsy is sometimes there, of course, and so is humor (a gift these critics sadly seem to lack). Surely there is an element of mortal panic and fear underlying all works of art?" (143–144). While elsewhere explicitly separating herself from "feminists," Bishop here defends Moore as an authentic "feminist," more courageous than those who would criticize her. What Bishop admires, among other elements in Moore's work, is the direct treatment of issues that the feminists themselves have deemed important: "Have they really read 'Marriage,' a poem that says everything they are saying and everything Virginia Woolf has said? It is a poem which transforms a justified sense of injury into a work of art." One should not overlook the self-revelatory terms in which Bishop couches her approval of Moore's personal and aesthetic choices:

> Perhaps it was pride or vanity that kept her from complaints, and that put her sense of injustice through the prisms dissected by "those various scalpels" into poetry. She was not too proud for occasional complaints; she was humorously angry, but nevertheless angry, when her publisher twice postponed her book in order to bring out two young male poets, both now almost unheard of. (144–145)

Noting the discontinuity between Moore's historical situation and her own, Bishop comments, "Now that everything can be said, and done, have we anyone who can compare with Marianne Moore, who was at her best when she made up her own rules and when they were strictest—the reverse of 'freedom?' " (145). The imposition of self-created rules speaks not only to Moore's poetic strategies (her use of syllabics, arbitrary rhyme schemes, and a defiantly idiosyncratic and demotically erudite diction); Bishop's comment also sheds light upon the motivations that inform her own use of poetic devices: her complex traditional forms, rigorously subtle rhymes, scrupulously delineated personae—the deflection of the personal through the adornment of narrative disguise. Bishop will, in both her poems and letters, reveal her preference for the defense of form. As she herself once remarked, "One can never have too many defenses." In poetry this conviction translates into verbal strategies that diminish the essential aversiveness of painful experience and allow the separation of the personal from the experience expressed. But in terms of sexual politics, such deflective strategies serve another, although related, purpose, that of masking any overt allusions to Bishop's lesbianism while consistently gesturing toward an erotic life that redefines as it obliterates conventional definitions of gender, and of sexual identity itself. Bishop reserves her greatest praise for Moore when she remains faithful to her self-imposed rules, a condition Bishop defines as freedom of choice.

In terms of Moore's and Bishop's overt, interpoetic relationship, a restrictive propriety seems to have prevailed:

> Sometimes she suggested that I change a word or line, and sometimes I accepted her suggestions, but never did she even hint that such and such a line might have been influenced by or even unconsciously stolen from a poem of her own, as later on I could sometimes see that they were. (145)

The generosity of Moore's sponsoring Bishop in *Trial Balances* (1935) is somewhat tempered, however, by Bishop's description of Marianne Moore's and Mrs. Moore's extended re-writing of one of Bishop's first long poems, a revision that altered stanzas, rhymes, and diction. Bishop records that in response to the Moores' suggestions, "I obstinately held on to my stanzas and rhymes, but I did make use of a few proffered new words. I am sorry to say I can't now remember which they were, and won't know unless this fascinating communication should turn up again" (146). The dismissive "fascinating" with its deflective irony suggests Bishop's need to defend against the remembered rejection, as well as her difficult assertion of independence from the Moores' combined judgment. Textually, Bishop resolves this tension by invoking a shared criticism of Yeats, a criticism that goes against conventional opinion and reveals something about the implicit feminism of both Bishop and Moore.

Bishop recalls that "Marianne in 1940 gave me a copy of the newly published *Last Poems and Two Plays*, by William Butler Yeats, and though I dislike some of the emphasis on lechery in the poems and so did she, I wrote her that I admired "The Circus Animals' Desertion" and the now famous lines "I must lie down where all the ladders start, / In the foul rag-and-bone shop of the heart" (146). The allusion to lechery once again points to the role of the moral and sexual in aesthetic judgment. Equally significant is the implicit existential standard Moore invokes when assessing Yeats' limitations; her articulation of what is lacking in his poems tells us what she expected from her own.

> I would be "much disappointed in you" if you *could* feel about Yeats as some of his acolytes seem to feel. An "effect," an exhaustively great sensibility (with insensibility?) and genius for word-sounds and sentences. But after all, what is this enviable apparatus for? if not to change our mortal psycho-structure. (146)

Technique should, Moore makes clear, be in the service of a change that extends beyond the aesthetic to life itself.

III

The circus, the movies, Coney Island—places of entertainment, diversions from the "ordinary"—provide the primary occasions for Bishop's anecdotes, creating an oddly aberrant vision of the childlike and the grotesque that invites us to view Moore almost as a caricature of herself. Hers is a life characterized by a prevailing, antiquated conservatism punctuated with excursions into a surreal world of exaggeration that taps or releases energies otherwise repressed. Bishop's descriptions of such diverting entertainment, moreover, re-introduce themes of gender identity through the guise of amusement. In "Some Expeditions," Mrs. Moore, deciding that the adult Marianne needs a diversion, takes her to Coney Island. There Marianne and her mother watch Sheba, "an unusually large and docile elephant," perform. When Bishop asks Moore about the elephant's appearance, her response completely ignores the fact that she is describing an *animal* and not a woman, a peculiarity silently

34

underlined by Bishop's transcribing the description without
adding a word.

> I asked about the elephant's appearance, and Marianne said, "She
> was very simply dressed. She was lightly powdered a matte rose
> all over, and wore ankle bracelets, large copper hollow balls on
> her front legs. Her headdress consisted of three white ostrich
> plumes." (147–148)

One notes the specificity of the description and its gender-
inflected language, yet, rather than comment, Bishop shifts to
the amusement park's other sites:

> Marianne was fond of roller coasters; a fearless rider, she pre-
> ferred to sit in the front seat. (147–148)

The sudden rush of sensation and the release of libidinous energies through the artificially induced pleasures of controlled and
delimited danger are the probable sources of Moore's pleasure.
During the ride, Moore's long red braid comes undone and her
amber-colored "real tortoiseshell" hairpins fall into the laps of
two sailors in the car behind her. That the pins fall into the sailors' laps is both fortuitous and suggestive. "At the end of the
ride, [the sailors] handed them to her 'very politely' " (148). The
distinctly masculine "sailors" meet their match in Moore, who,
whenever Bishop describes her encounters with such men (a
taxi driver, the administrator of her driving-test whom Moore
calls a "policeman") tames "male" aggression through the imposition of exaggerated civility or her sheer dignity of manner.

Issues of gender, sexual identity, and sublimation again
emerge in the description of Marianne Moore's tango lessons, a
subject introduced apparently to confirm Moore's curiosity and
taste for adventure. The care with which Bishop at once desexu-
alizes a rather alluring, consciously staged dance while emphasizing the language of gender foregrounds Moore's problematic
relation to her own sexuality. "The young dancers, male and
female, may have been a little surprised, but soon they were
competing with each other to dance with her" (149). The fact
that *male* and *female* dancers compete to have Moore as their
partner effectively declares her competence as Bishop's phrase
sexually neutralizes by echoing Moore's own gender-inflected
description, "she had also learned several other steps and

dances in more current use, and insisted everyone had enjoyed himself and herself thoroughly" (149). Here Bishop anecdotally re-asserts a hierarchy of values and a mode of conduct that characterizes the entire memoir: Moore's belief that practicality, curiosity, and common sense can domesticate desire, and that the combination of an ethics of conduct and the determined pursuit of staged "adventures" can delimit sexuality itself. The restrictiveness of this vision and the extent of Moore's denial inform her decisions regarding which movies she would not see or once having seen, would denounce, whereas Bishop distinguishes herself as again more worldly, more knowing, hence capable of assessing the limitations of Moore's point of view. "I never attempted to lure her to any dramatic or 'artistic' films," she recalls. "Since Dr. and Mrs. Sibley Watson were her dearest friends, she must have seen his early experimental films, such as *Lot in Sodom*" (a title suggesting sin, knowledge, and perversion) (151). When two young men take Moore to see Eisenstein's *Potemkin*, what captures her attention is a Walt Disney film that had "charm and humor." "Finally they asked her what she had thought of *Potemkin*. Her opinion was brief but conclusive: 'Life,' she said, 'is not like that' " (151). Again Bishop reveals the limitations of Moore's vision as well as her apparent inability to incorporate or even to come to terms with anything that lies outside her chosen sphere.

The exclusion of a specifically historical, as well as a sexually-informed, knowledge finds its corollary in Moore's attitude toward psychoanalysis. Here the difference between Moore's point of view and Bishop's is brought into sharp relief; Bishop's confiding to Moore that she had been seeing a psychoanalyst marks "one of the very few occasions on which we came close to having a falling out" (155). Moore's argument against psychoanalysis is a moral one, again indicating the circumscription of her imaginative life. Bishop writes, "She disapproved quite violently and said that psychoanalysts taught that 'Evil is not *evil*. But we know it *is*' " (155). Here, Bishop does stop to defend herself, an indication of the serious divergence of their views. As we have seen, conflict in Bishop's memoir does not characteristically provoke verbal refutation but rather denial, or acquiescence, as if Moore's and Bishop's relationship or Bishop's perception of it could not withstand the open pursuit of difference.

Bishop thereby remains the "good" daughter whose independence from the controlling, dominant mother signals a pain that
might injure or initiate the loss of the mother/mentor/friend
herself. The tenuousness of such a maternal relationship can be
translated into terms of "loyalty," but it is loyalty maintained at
a very high price.

To a woman who herself only experienced her original
mother intermittently and often apparently in states of emo-
tional collapse, what in her adult years Bishop discovers in
Moore is a surrogate maternal figure who re-enforces Bishop's
sense of familial exile. In her descriptions of Moore, Bishop
conflates the image of a controlling maternal presence with that
of an overprotected, sexually uninitiated child. In her worldliness, her modernity, her openness to experience, Bishop in one
sense consigns her mentor to a subordinate position, thereby establishing grounds for a condescension that enables her to distinguish and so separate herself from a mother who had never
been able or apparently never desired to separate herself from
her own mother, thus preserving Moore's anomolous status as
a mother-child. For, what Moore most obviously does not create
as an adult is a family of her own, and, as a consequence, the
issue of the conduct of life outside such a renewed family itself
acquires the aura of the problematic. The question of morality,
of how to conduct one's life without the biologically constructed
constraints of familial patterns and responsibilities, is one subject Moore openly confronts. Bishop gives the subject a paragraph, although the implications latent in Moore's observation
absorb the closing pages of the memoir as they inform Bishop's
recollections of Moore in their entirety. Bishop recalls,

> She once remarked, after a visit to her brother and his family, that
> the state of being married and having children had one enormous
> advantage: "One never has to worry about whether one is doing
> the right thing or not. There isn't time. One is always having to go
> to market or drive the children somewhere. There isn't time to
> wonder, 'Is this *right* or isn't it?' " (154)

Freed from the constraints of such obligations, the inhibiting
structures of maternal responsibility, Moore can fashion her
own priorities and yet, as Bishop writes in another context, *"the
choice is never wide and never free."*[12] Bishop comments,

Of course she did wonder, and constantly. But, as in the notes to her poems, Marianne never gave away the whole show. The volubility, the wit, the self-deprecating laugh, never really clarified those quick decisions of hers—or decisive intuitions, rather—as to good and bad, right and wrong; and her meticulous system of ethics could be baffling. (154–155)

What follows is Bishop's recounting of her confrontation (if one can call it that) with Moore over the issue of Bishop's analysis, but what the preceding observations reveal is Moore's inadequacy as a mother—the extent to which she was unable or unwilling to convey to her literary "daughter" a firm sense of values, limits, or a consistently generous ethical point of view. Moore leaves her daughter baffled, one surmises, because of her own need for self-protection. Charming as it may sometimes be, such rigidly erratic maternal behavior can create in her daughter confusion about life, priorities, and, finally, reality itself. What follows in the memoir's closing pages constitutes a coda which, although presented as a digression, is absolutely germane to the themes of mothering, chastity, and the hidden aggressions of the "Family Romance" already elaborated in the essay's preceding pages.

To provide a graceful rhetorical summation for her apparently benign, although deeply vexed, portrait of Moore, Bishop introduces Gerard Manley Hopkins' famous letter advocating the values of the gentleman over those of the poet.[13] Invoking Hopkins' judgment to summarize Moore's position, Bishop at once overtly extols Moore's aesthetics and ethics while, at the same time, noting the arcane and gender-inflected terms in which Hopkins expresses those values. Thus Bishop underscores in the very act of praising Moore the grounds for difference that have remained present although submerged throughout the essay. "Today [Bishop remarks] his ideas may sound impossibly Victorian, but I find this letter still applicable and very moving" (155). What Bishop then goes on to cite is Hopkins' plea for the superiority of a *moral purity*, or what he calls

that *chastity of mind* which seems to lie at the very heart and be the *parent of all good*, the seeing at once what is best, and holding to that, and not allowing anything else whatever to be even heard pleading to the contrary. [italics mine] (155)

To be this kind of "gentleman" is the lesson Moore would teach Bishop, but it turns out that a life thus lived is severely privative; and "chastity" cannot, in reality, "parent" anything. It is more important, Bishop avers, in Moore's scheme of things, to be a "lady" or a "gentlewoman" than a poet.[14] Although sensitive to the difference between the antiquated, gendered locutions that make "us uncomfortable now," Bishop nevertheless associates Moore's values with such an arcanely gendered chastity. But the memoir's tentative moral does not altogether suffice, as the final paragraph draws us back into further complexities rather than forward into the more limited perfection of the life Bishop has ostensibly chosen to praise. The earlier bafflement reasserts itself, and this, I would suggest, has less to do with Bishop's self-avowed difficulty in summarizing than with the inherently baffling portrait of Moore Bishop herself has already drawn.

Musing on Moore's name, Bishop discovers that she cannot advance beyond the initial letter that multiplies rather than resolves/resigns itself into a conclusive meaning. The inconclusive, provisional quality of Bishop's final meditation upon Moore's "mono-gram" suggests its interpretive impenetrability. Singular, distinctive, unique—how to pass beyond these associations to a synthesis of morality and manners, of self and other? "I have a sort of subliminal glimpse of the capital letter *M* multiplying. I am turning the pages of an illuminated manuscript and seeing the initial letter again and again: Marianne's monogram; mother; manners; morals" (156).[15] The "M" extends across Bishop's field of vision to cover the page, but unlike the "toils" of the "initial letter" upon which Bishop gazes in "Over 2,000 Illustrations and a Complete Concordance," the "M" does not resolve itself into clarity.

Bishop progresses as far as reading the "M" as mother, envisioning herself as the seven-year-old heroine of *Alice in Wonderland* and *Through the Looking-Glass*. For the mature Elizabeth Bishop to present herself as once again a young girl bemused by a manuscript that makes of manners and morals a mystery is both a regressive and a recuperative gesture. Only through the spectatorship of indirection can she make sense of her experience ("I catch myself murmuring"). The confusion at the center of Bishop's reading of the letter M, however, abides as the imaginary Alice tries to resolve her confusion: "Manners and morals; manners *as* morals? Or it is [sic] morals *as* manners?" "Since like Alice, 'in a dreamy sort of way,' I can't answer either question, it doesn't much matter which way I put it; it seems to be making sense" (156). But this "seems" introduces a doubt that cannot be dismissed by Bishop's characteristic gesture of effacement. For, despite (and because of) her enormous importance to Bishop, Moore remains deeply, inherently problematic. Moore's willfulness, desire for power, and attempt to control her refusal to come to terms, at least overtly, with sexuality, history, or contemporary secular life, create for Bishop overriding difficulties in determining if and how Moore's codes of conduct can be reinscribed in terms of her own experience. Yet, of course, these same difficulties enable Bishop to create a ground or basis for difference. The silences in "Efforts of Affection," the deflection of judgment, the repeated refusal to criticize, the representation of episodes without commentary, all bespeak an ambivalence too threatening to be directly addressed. As envisioned here, the mother is at once Romantic heroine, furtive animal, and pure artist of the unique. If Moore rejects the possibility of a literal maternity, she herself becomes, in Bishop's description, chaste mother as miraculous child. If Bishop, on some level, experiences Moore as a Virgin Mother, then the question is how simultaneously to contain, control, and emulate the miraculous?

To choose Moore as a literary mother has, of course, everything to do with the originality and brilliance of her poetic vision and what it might offer an aspiring woman poet. Bishop's choice is, therefore, gendered and deliberate, and yet it cannot evade the weaknesses of its strengths. For what one discovers reading "Efforts of Affection" are the lacunae that expose the difficulties of that choice, a striving to maintain affection in the face of a maternal will-to-power that would all but destroy the daughter-poet in the name of her empowerment. Although such a vision of the Family Romance is not new to psychoanalytic investigations of the mother-daughter relationship beyond Bishop's memoir, what one discovers within it is that the transferential relationship between the literary mother and daughter is as complex and fraught with difficulties as that between literary fathers and their sons. In Bishop's relation to Moore, one may tentatively posit an alternative model of mother-daughter interaction that does not evade but rather confronts the specific anxieties of influence as they emerge in the lives of two of this century's strongest women poets. The war with the mother is, in this case, characterized by silence, by condescension on the part of the daughter, and by a questioning of just what the mother's life might signify or how it could serve as a model. Granted that Moore's idiosyncracies inform this relationship and render it inevitably "unique," what one observes is that to "look back through one's mother" is as troubling, as problematic, as be-musing as looking back through one's father(s), because, what one witnesses viewing this mother-poet is a "blurred" image, a distorted vision of sacrifice and psychic dismemberment, a vi-sion of the mother who dis-engenders herself for art. That such a radical renunciation could alone preserve Moore's sensibility suggests the extremity of her situation vis-à-vis patriarchal cul-ture as well as the male literary tradition. These issues are, moreover, crucial to the conduct of life as well as to the conduct of art; hence the muted message of "Efforts of Affection" is the horror that would have greeted Moore's awareness of Bishop's sexuality, her gendered desire. Unresolved in "Efforts of Affec-tion," and therefore perhaps responsible for that very sense of effortfulness, homoerotic desire remains a subject for the poems to explore. And it is precisely in Bishop's poems that Moore is transformed into an enabling, because subordinate, imaginative presence. But the Moore of the memoir remains inviolably unique, impossible to duplicate and disabling—someone who can be told only a partial truth because the whole truth of her daughter's identity would shock her into alienation. The imper-ative to be the good daughter is the burden Bishop assumes in her friendship with Moore, whereas in her work Bishop could sufficiently define herself against her controlling, censorious, domineering presence to create a poetry that does not itself evade but actively engages those very aspects of human experi-ence that Moore herself was forced to censor.

What silently echoes thoughout Bishop's memoir is the ap-prehension that if Moore knew the complete truth about Bishop she would greet it with disdain. And it is this censoriousness that Bishop incrementally presents in her descriptions of Moore's response to any sign of sexual "aberration." Indeed, Moore's censoriousness as delineated in the memoir surpasses conventional prudishness to assume the status of a preciosity of judgment that turns into a constantly censoring presence. The nice distinctions Moore invokes for the contextual propriety of the word "rump" reveals a confusing, convoluted system of meaning that depends upon a mutual understanding on the part of both speaker and audience—a privatization of communal language. Such convolutions surrounding sexual or corporeal terms are problematically presented as rationalizations veiled by/in clarity: "Marianne once gave me her practical rules for the use of indecent language. She said, 'Ordinarily, I would never use the word *rump*. But I can perfectly well say to Mother, "Mother, there's a thread on your *rump*, because *she* knows that I'm referring to Cowper's pet hare, 'Old Tiney,' who liked to play on the carpet and 'swing his rump around!' " (130).

What makes this otherwise censored term acceptable is a literary and zoological context that screens its more overt meaning. Violation is avoided by the assumed essential conspiracy of a deliberate mis-understanding that depends upon a mutual mother-daughter acquiescence. One is tempted to recognize in these dual strategies a characteristic of Moore's poetic language more generally, wherein the screens of zoological and natural description release otherwise threatening because too intimate human disclosures related to feelings of vulnerability and desire. Such verbal defense, when applied to standards of behavior or to ethical questions, sends confused and conflicting messages to her poetic daughter. Consequently, it is to the mother-daughter paradigm as exemplified both by Klein's *Envy and Gratitude* and the Moore/Bishop relationship that I now return in order to suggest a somewhat more de-idealized description of poetic influence based upon what Bishop herself has in "Efforts of Affection" so tellingly disguised.

IV

The opening sentence of Klein's text asserts the power of the earliest infantile experiences to shape both negative and positive feelings. Klein notes, "I arrived at the conclusion that envy is a most potent factor in undermining feelings of love and gratitude at their root, since it affects the earliest relation of all, that

to the mother" (176). Indeed, Klein emphasizes the "fundamental importance of the infant's first object relation—the relation to
the mother's breast and to the mother" (178). Interestingly, the
father as separate entity does not appear at all but "only as in-
corporated into the combined 'parent figure.' "[16] Along with the
particular and unknowable physical conditions of the fetus,
Klein ascribes major importance to the external circumstances of
the birth trauma itself and to patterns of feeding and maternal
attitudes toward the newborn. Without offering a full reading of
the book, I would emphasize Klein's description of the significance of the breast and how it is perceived by the infant in
formulating the child's and later the adult's attitudes of greed,
envy, and gratitude and, moreover, the transferential importance of this first experience throughout adult life. Klein's most
telling observations in relation to "Efforts of Affection" have to
do with trust, gratitude, gift-giving, and the confusion created
by the denying mother—all themes that, as I hope to have
shown, recur throughout Bishop's memoir.[17]

Writing on friendship and the capacity for trust, Klein links
these issues to the initial infant-mother experience:

> The infant can only experience complete enjoyment if the capacity
> for love is sufficiently developed; and it is enjoyment that forms
> the basis for gratitude. Freud described the infant's bliss in being
> suckled as the prototype of sexual gratification. In my view these
> experiences constitute not only the basis of sexual gratification
> but of all later happiness, and make possible the feeling of unity
> with another person; such unity means being fully understood,
> which is essential for every happy love relation or friendship.
> (188)

This situation is exactly what Bishop finds lacking in her relationship to Moore, for such complete trust or understanding is
constrained on every side by Moore's perceived narrowness of
cultural and psychological vision, her refusal to experience reality except on her own artfully controlling terms. Furthermore,
Klein relates this initial experience of trust to the preverbal stage
of life. "The capacity to enjoy fully the first relation to the breast
forms the foundation for experiencing pleasure from various
sources" (188). In this regard, one recalls the discretion Bishop
records in her conversations with Moore and her reluctance to

43

risk giving offence. What makes "strong envy of the feeding breast" such a powerful experience, in Klein's view, is its replicative and potentially devastating psychic effects. There are, she maintains, "very pertinent psychological reasons why envy ranks among the seven 'deadly sins.' " "I would even suggest," Klein continues, "that it is unconsciously felt to be the greatest sin of all, because it spoils and harms the good object which is the source of life" (189). The care Bishop exercises not to "harm" or to "offend" Moore as transferential mother vies with her desire for autonomy without full disclosure. Who she is, her own constitutive identity, would, from all indications, provoke rejection and censure, thus pushing away as well as mutilating the good breast.

In terms of feeling, such rejection results in a severe injury to both child and mother. As Klein notes, "the feeling of having injured and destroyed the primal object impairs the individual's trust in the sincerity of his later relations and makes him doubt his capacity for love and goodness" (189). Although I do not sense in "Efforts of Affection" a doubt concerning Bishop's own capacity for love and goodness, what I do recognize is the display of an intense reserve that delimits and severely restricts possibilities for intimacy. How apt, then, is the Kleinian maternal model for theories of poetic influence given the formal character of these relationships and their literary context? By way of an answer, I cite the length, importance, and devotion of the Moore-Bishop friendship as well as the internal verbal evidence from "Efforts of Affection" itself. Not only is Moore the initiatory presence who helps bring Bishop's poems to print, her work serves as a sign of what poetry by a woman might be, an alternative to the aesthetics of the male modernists who are Bishop's other obvious literary precursors. Moore initiates a tradition that Bishop identifies as distinct, powerful, and worthy of emulation, although emulation always with a difference.

The fear that one will take too much, fear of one's own greed is, of course, not only a psychic fear but a literary anxiety as well. One can, in this context, understand Bishop's characterization of Moore as a split, fragmented, repressed, somewhat antiquated "other" as a way of insuring difference, a means of rationing Moore's verbal gifts so as not to be consumed by them (and reciprocally destroying the mother's breast—the very source of those gifts). Especially pertinent in this regard is

Klein's discussion of oral gratification and genital desires in light of Moore's habitual need to be certain that she has her own food, and that she carry it with her. One recalls from "Efforts of Affection" the buttered brown bread at the circus or "her habit of secreting food"—the two boiled potatoes lying on the dresser in her friends' "exquisitely neat" house in northern Maine (148). A confusion between genital and oral desires may, in part, account for Moore's anxieties about nurturance, but whatever the case (and I do not intend a Kleinian analysis of Moore), the fact that Bishop chooses to include these explicitly oral peculiarities speaks both to her vision of Moore as nurturing mother and to the excesses and peculiarities of hoarding food that the bread anecdote conveys.

The subject of ingestion and the infant's attitudes toward the circumstances surrounding this process leads Klein to a consideration of "creativeness" that she herself constructs through a literary paradigm. What one fears, in Klein's model of psychic giving, is the envy that causes the "spoiling" of creativity itself through the mutilation of the mother's breast. In terms of influence relations, the mother's creativity must be protected at all costs from her infant's greedy instincts; learning how to balance the nursing relationship becomes the source of later patterns of giving (*indeed the true subject of literary influence could be understood as the capacity to give and to receive gifts*). The primary anxiety, in this view, would be that what one desires is excessive, hence destructive or wounding to the giver. Klein describes the process, alluding to that most gendered of texts in the Western poetic tradition, Milton's *Paradise Lost*:

> The capacity to give and to preserve life is felt as the greatest gift and therefore creativeness becomes the deepest cause for envy. The spoiling of creativity implied in envy is illustrated in Milton's *Paradise Lost* where Satan, envious of God, decides to become the usurper of Heaven. He makes war on God in his attempt to spoil the heavenly life and falls out of Heaven. Fallen, he and his other fallen angels build Hell as a rival to Heaven, and become the destructive force which attempts to destroy what God creates. This theological idea seems to come down from St. Augustine, who describes Life as a creative force opposed to Envy, a destructive force. In this connection, the First Letter to the Corinthians reads, "Love envieth not." (202)

Klein goes on to assert that in her psychoanalytic experience, "envy of creativeness is a fundamental element in the disturbance of the creative process" (202). Consequently, given the threat of envy as understood by Klein, the daughter poet (in this instance Bishop) must find a way to shield herself from the devastating effects of her own envy of the mother, an envy that, in Klein's view, leads to the "initial source of goodness" being spoiled and destroyed with the consequences of the "good object being turned into a hostile, critical, and envious one" (202). Bishop protects herself against such envy through her implicit yet consistent exposure of Moore's limitations disguised as wonder at her mentor's uniqueness. Through her already described narrative strategies, Bishop is able at once to admire Moore's eccentricity while denying her literary foremother the full power of a flesh-and-blood woman, a strategy that Moore first seems to have invented for herself.

Such a defense on the daughter's part does not, however, keep her from experiencing a fundamental and regressive confusion that manifests itself (no matter how beautifully) in Bishop's attempts to come to terms with Moore's impact upon her. Klein associates confusion with various psychological phenomena that result from the blurred distinction between the good and the bad breast (a blurring one recognizes in Bishop's extremely mixed, deeply ambivalent portrait of Moore). But more importantly, Klein suggests that confusion itself may be used to fend off envy as well as other destructive impulses (220). This suggestion is especially useful in understanding Bishop's typical method of retreat, the substitution of a benign if self-deflating gesture toward one's own inadequacy as a way of effacing or denying more aggressive or destructive feelings. But the confusion itself (following Klein's argument) can be interpreted as a covert accusation, for she asserts that the primal causes for such confusion are related to projective and introjective identification: "Distrust and fear of taking in mental food goes back to the distrust of what the envied and spoiled breast offered. If, primarily, the good food is confused with the bad, later the ability for clear thinking and for developing standards of values is impaired." This results, according to Klein, in "inhibitions in learning and development of the intellect" (221), just what would be most threatening to a poet attempting to live the life of the imagination.

Applying Klein's theoretical rubric, one can more clearly assess the degree to which Bishop protects her own sense of poetic and personal autonomy at the same time that she acknowledges Moore's influence. This influence, in its inherently transferential cast, reenacts the earliest mother-daughter relationship as it writes the script for any subsequent transactions between the other and the self. When the exchange of gifts becomes a verbal exchange, when issues of sexuality impinge upon literary friendship, then the full reserve of Bishop's defenses necessarily comes into play. "Efforts of Affection," as its name implies, is a series of attempts to overcome and to ward off the primary ambivalence of the generative mother-daughter relationship in order simultaneously to pay tribute to and confine the poetic mother. By the close of the memoir, when Bishop herself is wondering what precisely she has learned from Moore concerning the single poetic life, she realizes that the lessons are either confused or inapplicable. What rises to the surface instead is the bemusement of irresolution, the result perhaps of the vexed, censored relationship that the essay has, albeit laconically, portrayed.

Finally, if it is in her poems that Bishop discovers the means to grapple with her precursor, to break free from the restrictive limitations of such a disengendered poetics, "Efforts of Affection" bears the signs of the residual originatory conflict that initiates Bishop's difference. At the memoir's close, Bishop, by representing herself as the bemused, seven-year-old Alice, constructs a persona of self-protection. To be an innocent, prepubescent girl bemused by the complexities of her mother's mysteries is to reassert her innocence as protection against Bishop's own gendered, erotic, hence censored identity which "Efforts of Affection" has sought both to efface and to disclose. What must be censored—specifically, eroticized desire—re-surfaces in the poems and in this memoir through the engenderment of rhetorical figuration.

For all its anecdotal digressiveness, "Efforts of Affection" proves central to an understanding of Bishop's poetics to the extent that it explores, however furtively, the origins of Bishop's relation to Moore in the mother-daughter conflict that necessarily informs any woman-to-woman literary relationship. Translated into the rhetoric of style, Bishop's indebtedness similarly leads to her formation of an empowering difference. If Moore

47

turns toward a minute and painstaking observation of the natural in order to express her subjectivity, Bishop learns from that meticulous power of observation an equal clarity. Yet Bishop balances that clarity with an equally compelling motive—to substantiate the subjective eros of sensation. Thus, Bishop incorporates the erotic life of the self into her poems in ways that, while distinguishing her from Moore, might nevertheless themselves be read as efforts of affection that take her beyond as they simultaneously recall her forbidding yet fortuitously inimitable precursor.

Reading Bishop Reading Moore

In the midst of this desolation, give me at least
one intelligence to converse with.
Ezra Pound

We need not be told that life is never going to be free
from trouble and that there are no substitutes for the
dead; but it is a fact as well as a mystery that weakness
is power, that handicap is proficiency, that the scar is
a credential, that indignation is no adversary for
gratitude, or heroism for joy. There are medicines.
Marianne Moore, "Predilections," 132–33

I

I F, IN "EFFORTS OF AFFECTION," Bishop covertly delineates the conflictual relationship between herself and Moore, Bishop's poems articulate the significance of that conflict. The psychological ramifications of the anxious ambivalence that shadows Bishop's relation to Moore have a determinative corollary in the realm of trope and the rhetoric of style. The analysis that follows, therefore, attempts to show how the Moore-Bishop relationship was worked out in rhetorical terms so as to establish a transposition from psychoanalytic inquiry to aesthetics. Object-relations theory here becomes supplanted by the principles of intertextual reading; my hope is that this substitution is suggestive of the ways that psychodynamics inform style. Primarily, issues associated with gift-giving, what can be taken and what must be spurned, are translated into allusive echoes, variations, and telling re-formations that point towards the individuating differences that mark Bishop's poetry. I have selected works for comparison that deal with conflict, whether between the epistemological dangers of the world and the possibility of safety or the efficacy of silence in relation to the power of speech. Bishop may take from Moore the descriptive terms or psychological determinants for such moments, but she veers from Moore, re-defining her predecessor's "gift," by emphasizing the provisional insecurity that governs a world of separation, longing, and loss.[1] In terms of object relations, the maternal gift is converted into a substance that can be accepted only when the negativity in that formulation has been fully explored. That such a revision may represent the enabling illusion of the younger poet's imagination does not detract from the powerful dialectic in which Bishop's poems are engaged. Aware that such a recuperative gesture on the part of the daughter poet is at once a necessary and empowering fiction, one can begin to read Moore as Bishop read her, discovering through such intertextuality those qualities that Bishop valued both in Moore and in herself. Bishop's poetic decisions—what she borrows from Moore and what she rejects (as well as the freedoms she chooses to exercise)—delineate her conception of the purposes and possibilities of poetry, thus clarifying the origins of her poetic "originality."

I begin this discussion by summarizing Bishop's own attitudes toward Moore and the values, both poetic and moral, that Moore represented. That aggression should be a factor in their relationship comes as no surprise; what is more revealing is Bishop's insistence upon denying tension between herself and Moore. Indeed, she is taken aback when a close friend finds "An Invitation to Miss Marianne Moore" (a deeply ambivalent poem) less than generous.

> My best friend in N.Y. thought my poem about her was "mean" which I found rather upsetting because it wasn't meant to be & it is too late to do anything about it now, I'm afraid. (to Lowell, Wiscasset, Maine, June 30)[2]

Although I shall return to a reading of Bishop's "Invitation" at this chapter's close, I cite her remark here in order to record Bishop's surprise regarding the aggression so clearly manifested in her poem. Criticism of Moore's over-solicitousness as well as of her way of writing poems is suppressed, one speculates, to preserve the illusion of an unambiguous loyalty. Yet Bishop's apparent refusal to acknowledge the anger that lies just beneath praise falls away before a skepticism that voices itself as affirmation. This complexity of feeling manifests itself in Bishop's implicit condescension toward Moore's mannered assurance.

> Did you know that she did some campaign writing for Hoover once?—in 1929 or thereabouts. But sometimes I think that that dogmatism *works* in her poetry—sometimes of course, not. I think (a simple thought) she must represent reassurance to all the audiences who hear her—a kind of family-feeling, and that if you'll be good you'll be happy—combined with intellectual *chic*! But heavens, what a wonderful old age she really is having—and deserving. (December 2, 1956)

Although here the ostensible "audience" is a popular one, and dogmatism is associated with a slogan-like patriotism (a salve of false security that bestows fatuous self-approval); in other contexts, family-feeling and ethical assurance are qualities in Moore that Bishop most deeply values. When, toward the close of "Efforts of Affection," Bishop invokes Gerard Manley Hopkins' letter to Robert Bridges expressing a devotion to "virtue" over art in terms of the dynamics of the family, when chastity becomes a source of value, one learns the importance of such a conception for Bishop's own understanding of herself as a poet. Hopkins admires "that chastity of mind which seems to lie at the very heart and be the parent of all good" (155).

I have already discussed the origins, or possible origins, of the confusion Bishop faces trying to conclude her memoir on Moore, trying to sort out the proliferating M's that multiply into confusion rather than resolve into an ordered clarity: "Marianne's monogram; mother; manners; morals; and I catch myself murmuring, 'Manners and morals; manners *as* morals? Or it is [sic] morals *as* manners?' " But I want at this point in my argument to introduce another, less overt possibility for Bishop's contemplation of the relationship between manners and morals, a source much more muted but nonetheless suggestive in terms of a maternal paradigm of influence. The phrase "Manners and Morals" echoes not only the Hopkins letter but a poem by Emily Dickinson, a poem that Bishop herself marked in her copy of the 1955 Johnson edition of *The Complete Poems*.[3] The subject of Dickinson's text is the Biblical Abraham's willingness to sacrifice his son Isaac to prove his devotion to God. Poem 1317 describes

Abraham's willingness to sacrifice his child for faith, investing the text's concluding lines with a particular resonance in terms of familial dynamics, faith, and the power of conclusions to teach us how to live.

> Abraham to kill him
> Was distinctly told—
> Isaac was an Urchin—
> Abraham was old—
>
> Not a hesitation—
> Abraham complied—
> Flattered by Obeisance
> Tyranny demurred—
>
> Isaac—to his children
> Lived to tell the tale—
> Moral—with a Mastiff
> Manners may prevail.

Dickinson's bitter lesson of the survivor stands in stark contrast to Hopkins' idealistic assertion. In terms of understanding the Bishop/Moore relationship and its stylistic implications, this possible alternative allusion to Dickinson's poem may in some ways prove as revealing, or more so, as the fully elaborated reference to Hopkins. For Dickinson's poem describes the efficacy of manners as a means of deception over and against an inherently brutal God. The audacious image of God as a powerful watchdog is somewhat muted by the alliterative sequence: "Moral"/"Mastiff"/"Manners," but the lesson is deeply subversive; this is a fable that sharply revises its sacramental theme. Dickinson draws *her* "moral" rather than presenting morality itself as an option—and her lesson is that strategies alone suffice when one inhabits a world ruled by a God who lacks compassion. Although I would not insist that Dickinson is the primary echo at the close of "Efforts of Affection," her poem's constellation of terms and its inverse resemblance to Hopkins' phrase and intent are suggestive. What Dickinson recounts is a severe indictment of God: the primal scene between father and son that acquires the significance of the deployment of deception in the face of a brutalizing, superior, patriarchal power.

I would suggest, moreover, that Dickinson's image of this patriarchal primal scene has been re-gendered in Bishop's memory to inform her understanding of Moore's significance as an exemplary woman poet; in other words, the choice between morals and manners remains confusing precisely because the moral character of the world one inhabits, shadowed as it is by Dickinson's austere assessment, cannot be as clearly discerned as Hopkins or even Moore might wish. Thus Moore might be understood as deploying a mannered style to confront a world that remains, however much she would insist upon moral certainty, both confusing and potentially dangerous. Aesthetics fuses with morality as her conception of poetry becomes a way of being in the world. Moore thus devises a means of self-presentation through composition that is based upon an ideology embodying the values of "humility, concentration, and gusto"—a performative disavowal of overt power that itself becomes a potent defense. Bishop, facing a related danger, acknowledges her confusion while absorbing and transforming Moore's poetic style.

One aspect of this style is a fidelity to the actual combined with a non-appropriative vision that respects modest observation above overtly performative assertions of power. "Integrity" remains at the core of Moore's understanding of her own ethical aesthetics, not so much constituting a confirmation of the status quo as a severe and radical indictment of it. Yet such "fidelity" or "truthfulness" may itself, of course, contain an element of self-deception—a fact of which Bishop is aware. When Bishop explicitly compares herself and Moore vis-à-vis the issue of fidelity to actual observation, she voices her admiration of Moore's capacity for such deception while at the same time invoking her predecessor's penchant for accuracy as a source for her own. Evaluating Lowell's poem "Water," Bishop draws his attention to the issue of pure fact:

> I have two minor questions, but, as usual, they have to do with my George-Washington-handicap—I can't tell a lie even for art, apparently; it takes an awful effort or a sudden jolt to make me alter facts. Shouldn't it be a *lobster* town, and further on—where the *bait, fish for bait* was trapped (this is trivial, I know, and like Marianne, sometimes I think I'm telling the truth when I'm not). (letter to Lowell, Rio de Janeiro, April 4, 1962)

The ascription of self-deception to both herself and to Moore, as well as the reference to George Washington, suggests Bishop's awareness of her own fallibility as well as Moore's in regard to the very issue of accuracy that remains at the core of both poets' stylistic principles.

Moore's self-created possibilities for poetry constitute a difference that Bishop herself associates with the subject of gender, a difference that acquires the attributes of a style. First note Bishop's telling, albeit extremely brief, comment above the title of Moore's essay "Humility, Concentration and Gusto."[4] Here Bishop reveals what she considers distinctive about Moore and the primary fact of this difference. She writes, "In itself—& as a comment on MM—the difference—(Eliot—Auden, etc.)." What this note confirms, and what Bishop's more extended comments on Moore reflect, is that, to Bishop, her predecessor represents a form of modernism that she perceives as distinct from that of the major *male* modernists. What Moore offers Bishop is not only an individuating ethics of style but the courage of that difference. Here is Bishop complimenting Lowell on his perception of Moore's revolutionary significance.

> What you say about Marianne is fine: "terrible, private, and strange revolutionary poetry. There isn't the motive to do that now." (June 25, 1961)

Although admiring Lowell's assessment of Moore, Bishop rejects his pessimism regarding the possibility of continuing or re-creating such poetry in the present, preferring instead the Emersonian injunction that "each new age requires a new confession, and the world seems always waiting for its own poet." Commenting upon Lowell's sense of motivation lost, Bishop speculates,

> But I wonder—isn't there? Isn't there even more—only it's terribly hard to find the exact and right and surprising enough or unsurprising enough, point at which to revolt now? The beats have just fallen back on an old corpse-strewn or monument-strewn battle-field—the real protest I suspect is something quite different— (If only I could find it. Klee's picture called FEAR comes close to it, I think . . .). (June 25, 1961)

Bishop's association of Moore with a revolutionary poetry of protest, as well as her perception that Moore provides an alternative to the male modernists, establishes her centrality to Bishop's own alternative quest. Articulating her allegiance through the guise of admiration, Bishop contemplates the very nature of the contemporary.

Expressing her thanks to Lowell for sending her a Webern recording, Bishop spans artistic genres for a definition of the truly contemporary, a definition that in itself defines the essence of Moore's poetics:

> they seem (the Webern compositions) exactly like what I'd always wanted, vaguely, to hear and never had, and really "contemporary." That strange kind of modesty that I think one feels in almost anything contemporary one really likes—Kafka, say, or Marianne, or even Eliot, and Klee and Kokoschka and Schwitters . . . Modesty, care, *space*, a sort of helplessness but determination at the same time. Well, maybe I'm hearing too much. (an admission of final ignorance!)
>
> (January 29th, I think—1958, I know)

Although in her later letters, as well as in "Efforts of Affection," Bishop presents a more antiquated and in many ways a more troubled evaluation of Moore, here she identifies her precursor with the contemporary that she herself would re-invent. As Bishop transposes Moore from contemporary exemplar to a figure of the modernist past and so places Moore in that past, Bishop constructs her own version of the contemporary through the deliberate and masterful choices that inform her own individuating style. This difference, as I have elsewhere suggested, is associated with Bishop's intense subjectivity, the presence of the erotic, and the poems' "natural" conversational tone—the willingness to sustain the provisional over Moore's yearning for closure. Moore's sense of effortfulness, the reaching for effect, falls away before an illusory descriptive ease, a subtlety that refuses to call attention to itself.

Commenting upon her and Moore's relative "difficulty," Bishop writes, "I can't imagine being *taught*—I'm so easy— however, one student at the Un. of Mass. (a friend taught me there wrote that perhaps "Sestina" was the name of my grandmother . . . & another that in the "Armadillo" the animals and I had had 'an experience none of them wd. ever forget. . . . ' I shod. tke about 1/10th as long as M. Moore, however—" (postcard to Sandra McPherson and Henry, dated Dec. 30).[5] Despite Bishop's assessment of her own "simplicity" compared to Moore's more overt difficulty (a completely illusory simplicity, to be sure), Bishop's poems engage equally problematic questions of style as they reveal their own investment in the poetic and philosophical questions that interested Moore. That Bishop resolves or experiments with different techniques only confirms the necessity to invent her own rhetorical solutions to mutually vexing questions. Reading Bishop reading Moore, one discovers what Bishop's poems themselves express, that Bishop is among Moore's most attentive readers. Thus reading Moore through Bishop, one uncovers a possible explanation for the digressive tactics of Moore's work as well as a surer sense of Bishop's own poetic strategies, for Bishop's reading illuminates her predecessor's poetry as it makes possible a more explicitly gendered and inherently less programmatic interpretation of Moore herself. Aesthetically, the two poets seem to share nothing less than a vision of the world.

On the most literal level, when one checks Bishop's own volumes of Moore's prose, one discovers Bishop's reiterated admiration for the values of simplicity, clarity, and unpretentious devotion to the actual that characterize Moore's observations. The motive for writing, Moore's motive for metaphor, is, furthermore, one that Bishop shares. In her copy of *The Marianne Moore Reader*, Bishop underlines the following:

> One writes because one has a burning desire to objectify what it is indispensable to one's happiness to express. ("Idiosyncrasy and Technique," 169)[6]

But the effort of such expression involves the overcoming of an innate reserve that would prefer an escape into obscurity equal to an immoral aesthetics:

> When obscurity was deplored, one should be as clear as one's natural reticence allows one to be. (171)

Although considering Moore's capacity to deploy descriptive language for deflective purposes, one might be tempted to read this ironically, I would suggest that such stylistic deflections prompt us to imagine the degree of reticence that Moore's rhe-

torical extravagance must have had to overcome. Such compre-
hension of difficulty informs another statement important to
Bishop: "When I am as complete as I like to be," writes Moore,
"I seem unable to get an effect plain enough" ("Humility, Concentration, and Gusto," 123). This ethics of composition, the aspiration to a poetics that would be at once unacquisitive and
accurate, informs both Moore's and Bishop's understanding of
what they would achieve, how they would define their individuating relationship to the world and to themselves in relation to
that world.

Yet, if, as I have been suggesting, this shared aesthetic inten-
tion assumes different guises in each poet, then one way of assessing the terms of that difference is to examine Bishop's rather
explicit verbal echoes of Moore and to observe as well how she
modifies Moore's psychological paradigms and rhetorical structures to accommodate her difference.[7] Although it may appear
initially rather naive to trace such verbal echoes and their variations, I do so to establish through circumstantial evidence just
how Bishop's language derives from Moore's and the linguistic
transformations that inform Bishop's stylistic distinctiveness.
Most striking in this regard are those moments when lines in a
Bishop poem seem to elaborate upon a passage from Moore and
then, through a shift in tone or meaning, release Bishop from
Moore's self-imposed verbal or psychic constraints. Consider,
for example, the closing lines of Moore's "The Hero" and
Bishop's "Over 2,000 Illustrations and a Complete Concordance." First, Moore:

> Moses would not be grandson to Pharaoh.
>   It is not what I eat that is
>   my natural meat,
>   the hero says. He's not out
>   seeing a sight but the rock
>   crystal thing to see—the startling El Greco
>   brimming with inner light—that
> covets nothing that it has let go. This then you may know
> as the hero. (9)

Unconstrained by the poem's decisive closure with its final
rhyme of "go" and "hero," Bishop incorporates the preceding

luminous image into the closing lines of her poem. Unlike the sightseer, who, through his acquisitiveness, violates what he observes, the hero looks with another kind of vision, with a generosity that will not convert observation into a form of property, "that covets nothing that it has let go." Is Moore's understanding of heroic vision not also the vision that Bishop desires when she opens the "book" at the close of "Over 2,000 Illustrations," a poem that itself engages the distinctions between sacred and profane sight, presenting experience as a way of reading the world as one travels through it?

Admonishing herself for having been the tourist Moore has disparaged, Bishop discovers in the pages of the sacred book a possibility for defining a different heroic vision—one that depends upon the power of the written word for this privileged relationship to its sight/site. And yet Bishop's exclusionary distance from the scene, from the illustration of the nativity, affords her access to what otherwise eludes her in her physical travels. Here is the passage that recalls as it revises Moore's:

> Open the heavy book. Why couldn't we have seen
> this old Nativity while we were at it?
> —the dark ajar, the rocks breaking with light,
> an undisturbed, unbreathing flame,
> colorless, sparkless, freely fed on straw,
> and, lulled within, a family with pets,
> —and looked and looked our infant sight away.

In these lines (as in the close of Moore's poem), one witnesses a luminous vision that is both inward and non-appropriative, that does not "use up" anything but rather glows freely in the dark. One recognizes Moore's cadences in Bishop's lines: the "startling El Greco brimming with inner light" now transformed into "the dark ajar, the rocks breaking with light." Crucially, these poems, despite their mutual divergences, identify a single source of light for praise. What constitutes the hero's vision in Moore's poem is that it "covets nothing that it has let go." In Bishop's poem, this becomes a somewhat more complex vision that, through its prolongation by repetition, introduces another level of irony. Bishop writes: "and looked and looked our infant sight away," staring into the scene and continuing to look beyond that staring until the silence of infancy falls away before the greater, more profound innocence of speech.

Throughout Moore's poems the need to defend the self and the essentially non-aggressive cast of that self become the dominant issues seeking an aesthetic resolution. The deployment of resistance as a means of forging ahead in the world conveys the self's precariousness as well as the world's inherent dangers. Such an adversarial yet non-aggressive vision of how to live and how to write, the challenge of a courageous modesty in the face of the obduracy of an always potentially menacing world, defines Bishop's as well as Moore's poetics. Although an awareness of the world's dangers does not stifle a capacity for enjoyment, it does render such enjoyment tenuous, subject to the need for exercising excruciating care. The opening of Moore's "Pangolin" might serve as an example of the self-conscious awareness of this treacherously repetitious situation. Tension between the need to defend and the essentially non-aggressive character of the vulnerable self is embodied in a creature whose function is not to render complex subjectivity more accessible but, rather, to make it that much harder, and hence, paradoxically, easier, to comprehend. As if recognizing her imagination's penchant for repetition, Moore acknowledges her own rhetorical and self-defensive strategy as she greets her subject—"another armored animal."

Interestingly, Moore's pangolin bears a distinct resemblance to Bishop's man-moth in its need for defense. Yet one of the qualities that separates the two creatures is that the man-moth is *not* armored against his own vulnerability, whereas the anatomy of Moore's pangolin offers protection. The pangolin, a structurally defended animal, makes its way through experience to welcome, despite the enormous resistance of the external world, an empowering reciprocity with the external, the morning, the power of the sun "that comes into and steadies (his) soul" (120). Moore thereby creates a being whose anatomical and skeletal characteristics in and of themselves become the occasion for defining a human relation to the world as they make that relationship possible.

59

... This near artichoke with head and legs and
                                    grit-equipped gizzard,
    the night miniature artist engineer is,
        yes, Leonardo da Vinci's replica—
            impressive animal and toiler of whom we seldom hear.
        Armor seems extra. But for him,
            the closing ear-ridge—
                or bare ear lacking even this small
                eminence and similarly safe

    contracting nose and eye apertures
        impenetrably closable, are not;—

With an anatomy constructed to protect his vulnerability, the pangolin forays into enemy territory and, like Bishop's mammoth, endures:

                ... —a true ant-eater,
    not cockroach-eater, who endures
        exhausting solitary trips through unfamiliar ground at night,
        returning before sunrise; stepping in the moonlight,
            on the moonlight peculiarly, that the outside
                edges of his hands may bear the weight and save the
                                                                claws
        for digging. Serpentined about
            the tree, he draws
                away from danger unpugnaciously,
                with no sound but a harmless hiss; ...

Whereas the pangolin's forays into unfamiliar territory are horizontal, close to the ground, buttressed by defense, the mammoth's similarly "exhausting and solitary nocturnal voyages" constitute an exilic quest of verticular investigation. Yet fear and an eerie moonlight shadow both the pangolin and the mammoth as they embark upon their perilous adventures. In Bishop's poem, however, the pangolin's protective armor—"scale / lapping scale"—has been stripped away, replaced by an anomalous, exposed being whose fluid cape itself signifies not so much a protection as that shadowy merger between creaturely and human consciousness.

              Here, above,
cracks in the buildings are filled with battered moonlight.
The whole shadow of Man is only as big as his hat.
It lies at his feet like a circle for a doll to stand on,
and he makes an inverted pin, the point magnetized to the moon.
. . . . . .

                But when the Man-Moth
pays his rare, although occasional, visits to the surface,
the moon looks rather different to him. He emerges
from an opening under the edge of one of the sidewalks
and nervously begins to scale the faces of the buildings.

"Scale" has in this context been transformed from the pangolin's protective armor into the active verbal signifier of escape by a partially human self so lacking in protection that he senses the moon's "queer light on his hands." Exquisitely sensitive to any fluctuation in temperature or to the absence of variation, the man-moth feels that the moonlight is neither warm nor cold— but "of a temperature impossible to record in thermometers." This world offers the man-moth no defense against his own vulnerability. Rather than taking solace in the moon as symbol or as natural source of light, "he thinks the moon is a small hole at the top of the sky, / proving the sky quite useless for protection. / He trembles, but must investigate as high as he can climb." The courage exemplified in the man-moth's explorations is that of breaking through into the unknown, into yet another vastness that promises no protection, an intensified experience of absence, of things as they are.

     Although the pangolin also makes exhausting solitary trips over unfamiliar ground, always returning before sunrise, his relationship to moonlight is one of avoidance as well as a constantly willed protectiveness:

              . . . stepping in the moonlight,
     on the moonlight peculiarly, that the outside
         edges of his hands may bear the weight and save the
                                                        claws
     for digging. . . .

He "roll (s) himself into a ball that has / power to defy all effort to unroll it." That defiant power stands in stark contrast to the man-moth's tentative extension of his body (with its attendant, fluid cape) into the void: "his shadow dragging like a photographer's cloth behind him." The black photographer's cloth imagistically functions as a fluent medium for protective disguise (like the paint, squeezed from a tube that colors what it touches).

If the man-moth's vertical efforts must end in defeat, the attempt itself constitutes its own logic.

> But what the Man-Moth fears most he must do, although
> he fails, of course, and falls back scared but quite unhurt.

That the man-moth sustains no real injury beyond his own fear reaffirms that the origins of his fear are so internalized as to render him provisionally "safe" either from externally imposed injury or defeat. Moore, on the other hand, deploys her pangolin's excursions to praise the wily facts of creaturely protection:

> Sun and moon and day and night and man and beast
> each with a splendor
> which man in all his vileness cannot
> set aside; each with an excellence!

Moore moves on to describe a confrontation between the pangolin and its prey in which the need for self-protection is matched by the necessity to obtain food. Whereas the pangolin is enacting its instinctual imperative, the man-moth's instinct immediately acquires a symbolic character—an entomological as well as tropological inheritance that impels the moth to fly into fire. But the man-moth's attraction to this light is a conflictual instinct that he at once, despite his desire, must enact, an impulse over which he struggles but repeatedly fails to win control.

> Up the facades,
> his shadow dragging like a photographer's cloth behind him,
> he climbs fearfully, thinking that this time he will manage
> to push his small head through that round clean opening
> and be forced through, as from a tube, in black scrolls on the light.
> (Man, standing below him, has no such illusions.)
> But what the Man-Moth fears most he must do, although
> he fails, of course, and falls back scared but quite unhurt.

Although "Man" knows better than to hope for victory in this quest, the man-moth's predicament is an utterly human one, for he struggles within and against the vertiginous desires that impel him toward confusion. Victimized by the uncontrollable speed of the trains he rides, he "always seats himself facing the wrong way," and "he cannot tell the rate at which he travels backwards." He is a creature of compulsion rather than of instinctual, unself-conscious confidence.

Consequently, the man-moth's gestures are the result not of affirmations of the will or instinctual self-preservation, but of obsession.

> Each night he must
> be carried through artificial tunnels and dream recurrent dreams.
> Just as the ties recur beneath his train, these underlie
> his rushing brain. He does not dare look out the window,
> for the third rail, the unbroken draught of poison,
> runs there beside him. He regards it as a disease
> he has inherited the susceptibility to. He has to keep
> his hands in his pockets, as others must wear mufflers.

The force of the imperative "must" conveys the man-moth's victimization before his unconscious as the "ties" suggest the repetition-compulsion that constitutes its origins; the man-moth must resist what amounts to an impulse toward suicide—a "genetic" weakness countered by self-restraint. Humanly attired—in a garment with pockets—he exercises an all-too-human effort against the self-destructive urge he otherwise cannot control. Despite verbal echoes and structural similarities, the man-moth and the pangolin each epitomize in their difference the radical turn toward subjectivity that defines Bishop's poetics from her predecessor's.

The pangolin's confrontation with his prey is as external and instinctual as Bishop's man-moth's confrontation is internal and excruciatingly self-conscious, for the pangolin mediates between getting what he needs, defending himself, and retreating in the face of a threatened counter-attack—his is the natural decorum toward which Moore would have us aspire.

> "Fearful yet to be feared," the armored
> ant-eater met by the driver-ant does not turn back, but

engulfs what he can, the flattened sword-
  edged leafpoints on the tail and artichoke set leg-and
                                  body-plates
  quivering violently when it retaliates
    and swarms on him. . . .

Employing the image of "the furled fringed frill on the hat-brim of Gargallo's hollow iron head of a matador" to describe the compactness to which the pangolin shrinks, Moore describes his retreat, emphasizing the absence of residual aggression and his resultant safety. "If" his natural adversary, the driver-ant, "swarms him," it will be met by retreat: "he will drop and will / then walk away / unhurt, although if unintruded on, / he cautiously works down the tree, helped / by his tail." "A thing / made graceful by adversities, con / versities," he is a survivor whose adaptability depends upon an instinctual physical tact that by displaying threat need not deploy it.

    Reading the final stanza of "The Man-Moth" in the context of "The Pangolin," one recognizes their related modulations. The syntactic resemblance between the "If . . . ," clause followed by the attribution of response—"he will drop and will / then walk away / unhurt" of "The Pangolin" is syntactically echoed in Bishop's lines: "If you catch him . . . " followed by her description of how the man-moth will respond:

    If you catch him,
  hold up a flashlight to his eye. It's all dark pupil,
  an entire night itself, whose haired horizon tightens
  as he stares back, and closes up the eye. Then from the lids
  one tear, his only possession, like the bee's sting, slips.
  Slyly he palms it, and if you're not paying attention
  he'll swallow it. However, if you watch, he'll hand it over,
  cool as from underground springs and pure enough to drink.

In her syntactically related description of the man-moth's "capture," Bishop implicates the readerly "you" in the drama of aggression, providing one with instructions on how to retrieve what the man-moth has to give, how to break through another's rather than (as in "The Pangolin") preserve one's own defenses. This readerly encounter describes the acquisition of a gift that takes from the man-moth his "only possession" presented as his sole defense. Through the attentiveness of observation, one can, without violence, win the man-moth's preciously defended tear, for the gaze itself, with the act of attention it implies, enables him to "hand it over." What the man-moth has to give and to give up is rare and pure, its value asserted by the conditions of the giving: through attentiveness and trust.[8]

If Moore's poem moves toward an ever-more-generalized description of the pangolin's generic status, Bishop's travels in the reverse direction, toward the intimate rendering of an encounter between the furtive, courageous man-moth and the reader her/himself. Moore's poem ends with admiration of the pangolin and confirmation of its power, a power that deploys rather than denies the creature's own fear:

> Not afraid of anything is he,
>   and then goes cowering forth, tread paced to meet an obstacle
> at every step . . .
> . . . .
> . . . The prey of fear, he, always
>   curtailed, extinguished, thwarted by the dusk, work
>   partly done,
>   says to the alternating blaze,
>   'Again the sun!
>   anew each day; and new and new and new,
>   that comes into and steadies my soul.'

A creature with a sense of humor and the necessary defenses for survival, the pangolin serves as an exemplum of that other mammal, "man."

The overt similarities between Moore's and Bishop's poems—allusions to the moon, the hat, the tentative, fearful, yet necessary explorations, the peculiarities of these respective creatures, the syntactically related closing descriptions of potential yet averted confrontation—gesture toward a more general distinction, as well as toward a difference between Moore's and Bishop's poetic sensibilities. Whereas Moore provides a strategy of defensive maneuvering that exemplifies how one might live within the limitations of an inherently dangerous world, Bishop, perceiving similar dangers and related limitations, chooses to describe the man-moth as a subjective being; what one witnesses is the pain he experiences as he tries to ward off his own self-destructive impulses. At the same time, "The Man-Moth" acknowledges the presence of a distinctive readerly "other" who would take something away—something priceless, extraordinary—something that strongly resembles the gift of art. If Moore endows "The Pangolin" with metaphoricity, anomalous personification, and a descriptive syntactical form, Bishop swerves from her precursor's text to probe the man-moth's status not as representational object designed for emulation, but as that imaginative being, oneself, who has something to offer if only one will bear with him. The trick is, of course, to find a way, non-aggressively, perhaps through an act of attention, to allow the man-moth (oneself) to relinquish and so share what he most defends and what therefore constitutes his "greatest beauty."

II

If Bishop shares with Moore a dislike of pretentiousness, ego-centricity, and performative self-display, theirs' is a mutual devotion to the values of freedom and the merits of privacy (see, for example, "In the Public Garden"). And surely it is this defensive modesty, the choice of willed self-effacement, that provides the strongest defense against a performative aesthetics that might otherwise make claims too portentous, claims that might provoke a potentially threatening response resembling envy.[9] Repeatedly, Moore associates the inherent dangers of explicit power with questions of literary style. As Bishop, surely one of Moore's most sensitive and intelligent readers, has in "Efforts of Affection" already made clear, for Moore literature is "a phase of life" ("Picking and Choosing," 45) and one must marshal one's defenses in order to live courageously or survive at all. The dangers for Moore, however, are somewhat different than for Bishop, and one can discern these differences by observing how each strives to counter what she conceives as most damaging to the "self." For Moore, too intense a self-scrutiny may result in confusion; suicidal dreams or self-inflicted injury can thus be avoided by turning outward, by humor and appreciation. Such a saving poetics resembles that of Bishop's "In the Village," which I discuss in this book's final chapter, where the aversiveness of the pain associated with the loss of the mother, her madness and intermittent (finally permanent) absence, is countered by a minute, lovingly detailed description not only of the blacksmith's shop but more generally of the particular objects that define the immediate, external world.[10] Too vigilant introspection, in Moore's view, leads to self-inflicted paranoia:

> ... you'll see the wrenched distortion
> of suicidal dreams
> go
> staggering toward itself and with its bill
> attack its own identity, until
> foe seems friend and friend seems
> foe. (35)

If Moore's "inflection" is often "disguised" (see "Those Various Scalpels," 51), it is not only because of her radical questioning of institutional structures but because of a more pervasive sense of alienation from the dominant and distinctly male-identified formulations of poetic modernism itself. Robert Lowell's recognition of the rebellion in her poems is absolutely accurate, for despite her many obscurities (or because of them) Moore takes her stand against self-posturing, against the Romantic mystique of self-divination. Her interrogatory poetics, although at times apparently in collusion with a male modernist tendency toward obscurantism, more often incorporates an open-endedness, a pluralism that eradicates hierarchy. Moore's presentation of a foreclosing aphoristic assurance lends her an enabling verbal authority that is quite different from Bishop's authorial voice. Whereas Bishop's voice may grow increasingly provisional, hesitant, or self-effacing as a poem progresses, Moore habitually forecloses the danger that her various voices will proliferate endlessly by seizing upon a moral or by giving what amounts to (or at least verbally resembles) a "prescription."[11]

If, in "Efforts of Affection," Bishop consistently draws away from the moralizing or summary phrase, it is precisely such gestures of closure that serve Moore as a necessary defense in her attempt to contain her rebellious, ever-accreting poems; such rhetorical gestures become a way of clarifying as well as disguising Moore's "ambiguous signature" ("Those Various Scalpels," 51). Her poems are clearly "products of the country in which everything is hard work" ("Snakes, Mongooses, Snake-Charmers, and The Like," 58), for to preserve pleasure over against the difficulties of making any progress at all requires of the reader an extraordinary act of attention. Such effortfulness may account for Moore's characteristic reserve, her drawing away from direct experience, her preference for the "post card" of the place rather than for the place itself. If, for Moore, travel is a means of secondhand observation (her vision of Brazil, like Dickinson's, would be that of the cerebral exotic), for Bishop travel offers the imaginary possibility of freedom. Bishop's capacity for direct contact as opposed to Moore's artistically mediated experiences marks a difference that speaks not only to each poet's understanding of her relationship to what lies beyond the self, but to Moore's and Bishop's conceptualizations of their relationship to the language that informs their poems.

Moore's "The Steeple-Jack" and Bishop's "The Unbeliever" each engage issues of safety and risk, the price of awareness, and the awareness of price as language serves to question the misrepresentation of safety in the world. Like many of Moore's most powerful poems, "The Steeple-Jack" is written from the perspective of an outsider, with an eye for the aesthetic of the place, an evaluative eye that seeks what will suffice for the imagination to feel at home. With an exactness that proleptically recalls Bishop's own acuity of vision, Moore describes "a reason for living in a town like this," which she associates with its aesthetic consolations as much as with its apparent security.

> Dürer would have seen a reason for living
> in a town like this, with eight stranded whales
> to look at; with the sweet sea air coming into your house
> on a fine day, from water etched
> with waves as formal as the scales
> on a fish.

Verbal control, enumeration, presentation of the "real" as a mimetic reproduction of life define this town transformed into art by the observer's gaze. And yet the fixed, definitional quality of the town described with such etched attentiveness gives way in the third stanza to a more emotionally mixed scene:

> whirlwind fife-and-drum of the storm bends the salt
> 　　marsh grass, disturbs stars in the sky and the
> star on the steeple; it is a privilege to see so
> much confusion. Disguised by what
> 　　might seem the opposite, the sea-
> side flowers and
>
> trees are favored by the fog so that you have
> 　　the tropics at first hand: . . .

Yet, despite the exquisite aspect of the floral display, this is not, the poem reminds us, an exotic terrain but rather the efflorescence of the domestic:

> but here they've cats, not cobras, to
> 　　keep down the rats. The diffident
> little newt
>
> with white pin-dots on black horizontal spaced-
> 　　out bands lives here; yet there is nothing that
> ambition can buy or take away.

Within this place, with its bracing air of the particular, Moore gives us a view of its three inhabitants—each human, each different:

> 　　　　　　　　　. . . The college student
> named Ambrose sits on the hillside
> 　　　　　with his not-native books and hat
> and sees boats
>
> at sea progress white and rigid as if in
> 　　a groove. Liking an elegance of which
> the source is not bravado, he knows by heart the antique
> sugar-bowl shaped summer-house of
> 　　interlacing slats, and the pitch
> of the church
>
> spire, not true, . . .

Not reading, but looking, the student knows the place, having committed to memory, learned "by heart," the individual details that define it. With a taste for elegance that stems from the opposite of bravado, he is indeed the student of the place that he both inhabits and views. What he observes when he looks at the church spire, "not true," is a "man in scarlet" who "might be part of a novel" except that he is not; he is, with the specificity of name and employment, "C. J. Poole, Steeple-Jack." Beneath C. J. Poole are two signs, one identifying the worker, the second issuing a warning, "Danger."

Like one of Bishop's Nova Scotian villages, the town has what one needs:

> The
> place has a school-house, a post-office in a
> store, fish-houses, hen-houses, a three-masted
> schooner on
> the stocks.

Here "the hero, the student, / the steeple-jack, each in his way, /is at home." Although Moore has earlier named the student and the steeple-jack, this is our first encounter with the "hero," who may be associated with an imagination at peace in its sense of a place so alluringly secure. And yet the poem's conclusion makes clear that the speaker-as-observer is a visitor not a native, that what she most admires about the town is an appearance of safety that masks just how dangerous this and every other place may be. Here one may be misled as to what to guard against, falsely reassured by the care others exercise who provide signs of danger even when they may not be needed.

> It could not be dangerous to be living
>   in a town like this, of simple people,
> who have a steeple-jack placing danger-signs by the church
> while he is gilding the solid-
>   pointed star, which on a steeple
> stands for hope.

In "gilding" the star that stands for hope, that both literally stands on high and symbolically represents aspiration, the steeple-jack also takes care of what is below him, aware of the possible dangers of his ropes and possible harm to others. He does not, however, protect one from the corruption that may reside within the church. "This would be a fit haven for waifs, children, animals, prisoners / and presidents who have repaid /sin-driven / senators by not thinking about them." *Danger* as a sign only externally protects C. J. Poole as well as the "simple" townspeople. Such knowledge of trepidation, the fear of anything beyond what can be controlled—beyond the realm of language as signpost of danger—may arguably inform the defensive linguistic strategies Moore devises to encounter an inherently treacherous world.

Like Moore's "Steeple-Jack," Bishop's "The Unbeliever" engages questions of doubt and belief, but here the focus is upon the imagination's awareness or blindness to the danger of all that lies both within and beyond it. Whereas Moore's steeple-jack places a danger sign where it may not be needed and avoids the corruption that lurks within, the "unbeliever" in Bishop's poem, himself in imminent danger, closes his eyes not only to that danger but to the efficacy of the very awareness of danger itself. Bishop's unbeliever is a voyager who discovers not in the external world but through his dreams what threatens to engulf him. Having relinquished the safety of Moore's seaside town, he is another "hero" in a dangerous world. For him, however, all action is internal; the man sleeping on top of the mast is also the sleeper in his bed, a dreamer confronting the terrors of his own imagination. As sleeper and introspective "look-out" man, the unbeliever lacks the steeple-jack's volitional and pragmatic relationship to the external world.

> Asleep he was transported there,
> asleep he curled
> in a gilded ball on the mast's top,
> or climbed inside
> a gilded bird, or blindly seated himself astride.

The repetition of "gilded" recalls Moore's steeple, but the purposive activity, the caution, the ropes and the red-and-white danger sign have all been replaced by somnolent passivity. Yet, as in Moore's poem, the reader recognizes three distinct imaginative alternatives that recall Moore's steeple-jack, student, and hero.

The three presences in Bishop's poem—the cloud, the bird, and the unbeliever—each confront the issue of ontological instability, of where to locate security in a world devoid of any absolute assurance.

71

"I am founded on marble pillars,"
said a cloud. "I never move.
See the pillars there in the sea?"
Secure in introspection
he peers at the watery pillars of his reflection.

Deluded by his own subjectivity, the ephemeral cloud, gazing at the reflected masts, mistakes them for foundations. The pillars (recalling the "four fluted columns, each a single piece of stone, made modester by white-wash") that had seemed so secure in Moore's poem, now are only proof of an illusion. In the gull's voice one hears this illusory solidity projected onto a vertiginous open space. In an effort to conjoin movement with stability, the deluded imagination again fuses an ambition for free flight with the yearning for assurance in a deceptive trope that finds no answering reality in what lies beyond the figural imagination. "Up here / I tower through the sky / for the marble wings on my tower-top fly." The multiple use of "tower" as self-generated movement and monumental artifact sustains the subjective illusion of safe flight. One notes the anxious differences between this gull's delusory subjectivity and the gulls that circle so regularly in "The Steeple-Jack"—birds that serve as external demarcations of natural order:

One by one in two's and three's, the seagulls keep
        flying back and forth over the town clock,
or sailing around the lighthouse without moving their wings—
rising steadily with a slight
        quiver of the body—or flock
mewing where

a sea the purple of the peacock's neck is
        paled to greenish azure . . .

Sailing around the lighthouse, Moore's gulls, borne up by air currents, preserve as they enact a natural rhythm. They fly back and forth over man-made objects which also bestow a measured order upon the world in the images of the town clock and the lighthouse. In this scene, natural rhythms work in harmony with the human artifacts that inform their surroundings. Unable or unwilling to give himself up to the hazards of flight, Bishop's

72

gull, living in no such world of measured accuracy, must construct a myth of support, a marble flying tower that externally will bestow upon him what he himself, in actuality, already possesses—the capacity for flight. Whereas Moore's gulls sail "without moving their wings," in Bishop's poem "wings" represent the effort that marks the gull's determined activity, the burden of carrying one's own, dense, marble air-column, the difficulty of transporting a tower in flight. But over against the cloud's and the gull's delusions (for both are false believers in stasis or external security) is the dream of the unbeliever who apparently remains oblivious to any external awareness of the risk he himself incurs:

> But he sleeps on the top of his mast
> with his eyes closed tight.
> The gull inquired into his dream,
> which was, "I must not fall.
> The spangled sea below wants me to fall.
> It is hard as diamonds; it wants to destroy us all."

This is the imperiled consciousness whose dream does not delude but rather confirms what he has closed his eyes to avoid, an external urge to destruction that is not individual but universal.[12] What the oblivious dreamer dreams is a vision of the danger that can only be confronted by such a blindly obdurate will, the determination of the human desire to survive. With its imagistic echoes of "The Steeple-Jack," that other man on high, Bishop's "Unbeliever" turns away from the delusory security of man-made signs identifying unreal dangers, the regulatory, warning functions of the town-clock and the lighthouse. Asleep one is on one's own as well as deeply implicated in the uncontrollable workings of the unconscious. If Moore does not make herself a citizen of the protective simplicity she creates, she nevertheless envisions herself as one who can at least provisionally imagine the security of such a place. Bishop, however, by taking us beyond the marginalization of the traveller into a sea of terror, confronts the subjectivity of unbelief that Moore in "The Steeple-Jack" would mediate through the protective guises of personal responsibility and the cyclic consolidations of the natural world.

Moore's strategy in "The Steeple-Jack" is to render the little town an already aesthetically formed artifact, more a postcard of a town than a town itself. Its reality has been translated before it is represented by the discipline of her aesthetic vision. But, while such prescriptive strategies of aesthetic control govern the ways that Moore directs the reader's vision, her more generalized conception of art is not so much to fortify the boundaries between poem and reader as to overcome readerly resistance, to make one yield one's defenses:

> to teach the bard with too elastic a selectiveness
> that one detects creative power by its capacity to conquer one's
> detachment, ("The Labors of Hercules")

Moore thus strives in her poems to maintain a poise between her own conception of aesthetic effectiveness and her impetus to disguise, transpose, or deflect the direct experience of human feeling. Arguably, this apparent conflict between the oppositional requirements of aesthetic power and poetic defense may arise from Moore's problematic understanding of her audience as well as from the requirements of a sensibility that must continually disguise in order to write. The reticence that marks her imagination can, therefore, be understood as creating a style that maintains a complicated dynamic between competing needs—the goal of evoking powerful emotion and the necessity of protecting, through verbal and metrical controls, the author's subjectivity.

Such tension between reticence and a spontaneous expressiveness is associated with Moore's conception of decorum and its relation to intimacy; of manners and morals, of how to conduct one's life, or more broadly, the ethical imperatives that inform style. In the light of these issues, I approach two poems that associate the powers of language and of silence with someone else's voice, in each case that of an older male relative; in Moore's poem, the voice of the father; in Bishop's, the voice of the grandfather. Each text, moreover, is explicitly didactic, presenting a moment recollected from childhood, in which the young girl learns about language and its "proper" role in bridging the domestic and communal spheres. Moore's "Silence" advocates an austerity embodied by the poem itself:

My father used to say,
"Superior people never make long visits,
have to be shown Longfellow's grave
or the glass flowers at Harvard.
Self-reliant like the cat—
that takes its prey to privacy,
the mouse's limp tail hanging like a shoelace from its mouth—
they sometimes enjoy solitude,
and can be robbed of speech
by speech which has delighted them.
. . . . . .

The deepest feeling always shows itself in silence;
not in silence, but restraint."
Nor was he insincere in saying, "Make my house your inn."
Inns are not residences.

In her father's definition of the "superiority" to which he clearly
aspires and which he would have his daughter share, people do
not impose nor do they depend upon seeing sights of more
general or "common" interest. They are, most importantly, self-
reliant. This self-reliance is, furthermore, presented in an amusing, homely, yet predatory image, for the superior individual is
compared to a cat that has just caught a mouse, its "shoelace"
tail dangling from the cat's mouth, a disquieting sign of its predatory powers. Not only do "superior" people "sometimes enjoy
solitude," but they themselves can become threatened by the
very words that have delighted them. Communication, no matter how pleasurable, potentially can destroy one's capacity for
speech. The solution would be total concealment—"the deepest
feeling always shows itself in silence, not in silence, but restraint." How the father's admonitory definition of "superior"
people affects his daughter is answered obliquely through syntax and the deployment of diction. In the phrase, "nor was he
insincere in saying, 'make my house your inn,' " the negative
conjunction "nor" and the attribution of "not insincere," convey
a diminished assertion of paternal sincerity that suggests a genuine hospitality on the father's part that only apparently contra-
dicts the negativity of his locution. Thus, the self-contradictory
syntax and diction simultaneously raise and answer the issue of
sincerity, pointing toward the disparity between such restraint

and a more generous hospitality. In emphasizing this difference, Moore verbally proves herself her father's daughter as the poem's own supposed clarification opts for a verbal restraint that complicates rather than simplifies his distinction. As a place one visits, usually as a paying guest, an "inn" both bestows and limits hospitality; thus "make my house your inn," a phrase which, in its original context, is an outright expression of Samuel Johnson's gracious, expansive hospitality, becomes a much more ambivalent invitation. The offer is to visit not to stay, to use his home but not to take it for granted, *not to feel completely at home in it*. Of the poem's two lines not attributed to the father, the final one, despite its brevity, is starkly revelatory, for it discloses Moore's awareness of the distinctions implicit in her father's choice of the "inn" and how this muted hospitality matches his conception of privacy and the need for restraint. But in choosing her own alternative to "inns," Moore herself selects "residences," a word of much greater formality, more forbidding than any inn might be. The words one would anticipate are, of course "homes" or even "houses"—with their associations of comfort and security. That Moore should instead choose "residences" is to enact the very qualities that her father has just extolled. If, however, one reads "residences" as an ironic choice that functions to preserve the father's terms while drawing attention to their inadequacy, then Moore may evoke in the reader a nostalgia for the unspoken "home" that the reader has already anticipated. Thus, the reader may experience a verbal disappointment that mimetically reproduces the authorial response to her father's severity—a response conveyed in the image of the isolated, predatory, "superior" self. In this reading, "residences" would therefore serve to underscore a silent criticism of the father's values. Furthermore, in a poem about speech and its absence, what that "superior" self carries in its mouth are not words but the dead prey on which it will feed. But, of course, this subtextual dialectic between paternal authority and the daughter's voice must be achieved through a kind of readerly attention that may discourage as it elicits interpretation. In its sparseness, its dispersal of point of view, its suppression of commentary or interpretation, and its non-human example (the humorous diminution of the "superior" father through the trope of the satisfied cat), Moore's poem reveals a characteristic strategy for dealing with a forbidding subject. Certainly the extent of a long-absent father's influence upon a poet who otherwise consistently emphasizes her mother's power might prove an occasion for such verbal logistics.

On the surface, Bishop's poem, "Manners," tells an apparently different story but with a similarly contradictory "moral." Beneath the title is one of Bishop's few dedicatory notes, "For a Child of 1918," a gesture both to the child and to the historicity determining that childhood. The fact that the dedication should emphasize the anonymity of the child (Bishop herself?) and the naming of the year further suggests the chronological limitations of the manners that the poem will take as its subject. The time is past, and these manners are appropriate to a child of another era; yet this is a child to whom the speaker still feels connected. What her grandfather teaches the child is an overt, expansive friendliness, "country manners," and a hearty warmth that rather than serving to reassure the child, actually awakens her anxieties and reveals the inadequacies of such expansive friendliness. The grandfather's manners are, moreover, outdated by contemporary circumstance: the noise and dust of the cars that pass by the wagon, passengers who never even hear the grandfather's and his granddaughter's greetings. The poem opens with a simple, grandfatherly injunction:

> My grandfather said to me
> as we sat on the wagon seat,
> "Be sure to remember to always
> speak to everyone you meet."

Following this advice, given in primer-style, is its application. He greets (as does she) a stranger on foot. "Then we overtook a boy we knew / with his big pet crow on his shoulder. / 'Always offer everyone a ride; don't forget that when you get older.' " The poem provides no commentary but a narrative that didactically conveys the importance of an endearing simplicity. When the young boy, Willy, upon the grandfather's invitation, climbs onto the wagon, his pet crow flies off. "I was worried. / How could he know where to go?" The child's question introduces a doubt that interrupts the pattern of easy assurance presented by the grandfather. Noting the crow's obedience and choosing it (recall the use of the predatory cat as emblem of the superior person in Moore's poem) as an example of proper behavior, the grandfather attempts to alleviate the child's fear: "A fine bird," my grandfather said, / "and he's well brought up. See, he answers / nicely when he's spoken to. / Man or beast, that's good manners. / Be sure that you both always do." But such politeness, the moral of the manner (and its concomitant arcane verbal reversal), is welcomed by a world harsher than the one the grandfather is prepared to meet:

> When automobiles went by,
> the dust hid the people's faces,
> but we shouted "Good day! Good day!
> Fine day!" at the top of our voices.

Shouting to faceless people amounts to a gregariousness that borders upon futility. The final instance of good manners, moreover, getting out of the wagon to lighten the mare's load, while endearing, displays a controlled generosity questioned as it is accepted in the poem's final "required." Like Moore's "residence," Bishop's "required" conveys an implicit comment upon values that are at once regarded with nostalgia and shown to have been rendered obsolete by the external realities of the contemporary world:

> When we came to Hustler Hill,
> he said that the mare was tired,
> so we all got down and walked,
> as our good manners required.

One senses, in the fulfillment of manners' requirement, just a hint of a seven-year-old girl's weariness. Although a much gentler and more generous view of relationships, of the world and of others, emerges from "Manners" than from "Silence," there is in both poems the recollection of a familial, authoritative male voice teaching a moral lesson. Whereas Moore seems to speak through the voice of the father while aware of the limitations and dangers of his prescriptive vision of superiority, Bishop affectionately tests her grandfather's more generous prescriptions against the circumstances of the day and, although without any overt criticism, suggests their limitations without diminishing that affection.

There are, of course, many other moments when one over-hears Bishop learning from Moore, echoing a cadence, or revis-ing an image to accord with her own "ambiguous signature." One thinks, for example, of Bishop's fish, the one she lets go, and sees in it the signs of age and of survival that one witnesses in Moore's, where "all / external / marks of abuse are present" ("Those Various Scalpels" and "The Fish"). Or one recognizes Bishop's cadences from "At the Fishhouses" ("It is like what we imagine knowledge to be: / dark, salt, clear, moving, utterly free . . . / forever, flowing and drawn, and since / our knowl-edge is historical, flowing, and flown") in Moore's "What Are Years?": "the sea in a chasm, struggling to be free and unable to be, / in its surrendering / finds its continuing." The freedom won through containment, the endurance that triumphs simply through survival, these we recognize as both Moore's and Bishop's values. Both poets share, moreover, a definition of the humble origins of happiness, the belief that "satisfaction is a lowly / thing, how pure a thing is joy" (95). One notes that a friend's report of reindeer in Lapland in Moore's "Rigorists" re-sembles Bishop's moose. Here is Moore's animal: "One looked at us / with its firm face part brown, part white—a queen / of alpine flowers" (96). Although Moore's reindeer's antlers are a baroque "candelabrum-headed ornament" and her poem turns toward the polemically engaged questions of the interrelated usefulness of animal and person, Bishop's poem captures the same initial moment of mutual recognition, the emotion awak-ened by the moose's sudden appearance, for her emphasis is on how she and others discover a moment of joy and then witness its vanishing. The opening lines of Moore's "Virginia Brittania" (107ff) serve as one source (along with Whitman's "Out of the Cradle") for the first stanza of "The Moose."

> Narrow herring-bone-laid bricks,
> a dusty pink beside the dwarf box-
> bordered pansies, share the ivy-arbor shade
>> with cemetery lace settes, one at each side,
>> and with the bird: box-bordered tide-
>> water gigantic jet black pansies—splendor; . . . (108)

And Bishop:

79

> From narrow provinces
> of fish and bread and tea,
> home of the long tides
> where the bay leaves the sea
> twice a day and takes
> the herrings long rides. ("The Moose," 169)

While Moore's lines veer into an ever-accreting descriptive-
ness where flourishing life coexists with a death-like excess,
Bishop's lines speak of separation, of leavetaking, a going away
from home designed into the very nature (the tides) of the
place.

Resemblances in style, theme, and tone proliferate, as when,
for example, the internal questions and tentative answers in "A
Carriage From Sweden": "A Dalen / light-house, self-lit—responsive and responsible" inform the modulations upon a single word in Bishop's "The End of March": "Everything was
withdrawn as far as possible, indrawn"; or, from the same
poem, "A kite string?—But no Kite." Reminiscent of Moore is
Bishop's offering a possibility as she withdraws it: "A light to
read by—perfect! But—impossible." At moments, too, a passage
in Moore may expand through Bishop's lines, as the close of
Moore's "A Face" (141) finds its elaboration in Bishop's sestina,
"One Art":

> Certain faces, a few, one or two—or one
> face photographed by recollection—
>   to my mind, to my sight,
>   must remain a delight. (141)

Bishop disperses Moore's enumeration of loss over two stanzas
as she converts the delight of recollection into the painful consolations of the survivor.

> I lost my mother's watch. And look! my last, or
> next-to-last, of three loved houses went.
> The art of losing isn't hard to master.
>
> I lost two cities, lovely ones. And, vaster,
> some realms I owned, two rivers, a continent.
> I missed them, but it wasn't a disaster. (178)

In each instance verbal resemblance modulates into Bishop's distinctive vision of separation and loss.

If Robert Lowell is correct (and I believe he is) when he asserts that Elizabeth Bishop is impossible to imagine without Marianne Moore, it may be that Moore herself uncannily becomes impossible to imagine without Elizabeth Bishop, freed as Moore is by her own strong reader. For if these poets share a world of the "always actually personal" (Moore, "In the Public Garden"), of the "illumined eye" (Moore, "Blessed Is The Man,"), a world of "unhackneyed solitude" (Moore, "Armor's Undermining Modesty"), and a belief that "the power of relinquishing / what one would keep; . . . is freedom" (Moore, "His Shield,"), they also most assuredly share a related and, in Bishop's case, transforming courage. What Bishop confirms for Moore is the possibility that "trust begets power and faith is / an affectionate thing." Difficult and vexed as Bishop's relationship to her most distinguished and influential precursor may be, the gifts she accepts from Moore are transformed into work that may offer possible "cures" for Moore's self-diagnosed "word diseases"—the need to encode, to distract through descriptions of prolonged accuracy, to defend through enumeration—all signs of a poetics inherently in conflict with itself. As Moore herself writes:

> I've escaped?
> am still trapped
>
> by these
> word diseases. ("Avec Ardeur," 238)

Evading Moore's apparent need for finding an aphoristic or slogan-like resolution to what must have seemed the overwhelming lure of the particular, Bishop sustains in her artfully natural voice the tensions Moore rhetorically encloses or aphoristically resolves. Bishop, by thus extending Moore's "limitations," discovers in her predecessor's works a resonant difference against which her own voice can be heard.

The most cursory glance at "Invitation to Miss Marianne Moore" reveals Bishop's recognition of Moore's enabling "limitations," for Bishop's poem is itself packed with that combina-

tion of abruptness and over-reaching artfulness that displays
Moore's poetic weaknesses masked as strengths.

> From Brooklyn, over the Brooklyn Bridge, on this fine morning,
>   please come flying.
> In a cloud of fiery pale chemicals,
>   please come flying,
> to the rapid rolling of thousands of small blue drums
> descending out of the mackerel sky
> over the glittering grandstand of harbor-water,
>   please come flying.

Too polite, and too much. The stage direction in the middle
of the next stanza: "Enter" and the subsequently elegant and
arcane description of the natural are more like Moore than
like anything in Bishop's own work: "two rivers, gracefully
bearing / countless little pellucid jellies / in cut-glass epergnes
dragging with silver chains." Not only is the diction uncharac-
teristically precious, Bishop's overt reassurances speak to her
awareness of Moore's anxieties: "The flight is safe; the weather
is all arranged" (as it was, we recall, in "The Steeple-Jack"). This
is the risk of the weather transformed by aesthetic control, into
a postcard, a rhetorical gesture reminiscent of Moore's own
poem. Bishop's description of Moore invokes a witch-like, an-
gelic precision, as it envisions Moore "with heaven knows how
many angels all riding / on the broad black brim of your hat."
Moore's "unique" ear, her monitory power, her censoriousness—all are noted in this invitation:

> Bearing a musical inaudible abacus,
> a slight censorious frown, and blue ribbons,
>   please come flying.

Bishop makes Manhattan "safe" for Moore: it "is all awash with
morals this fine morning." If it were not, Bishop implies, Moore
would not venture to where Bishop has already been and where
she now resides. In Bishop's anticipatory description of Moore's
wildly courageous flight (a flight signifying avoidance as much
as adventure), one witnesses Moore's inherent unsuitability to
the contemporary:

> Mounting the sky with natural heroism,
> above the accidents, above the malignant movies,

82

(the ones Bishop has avoided taking Moore to see),

> the taxicabs and injustices at large,
> while horns are resounding in your beautiful ears
> that simultaneously listen to
> a soft uninvented music, fit for the musk deer,
> > please come flying.

The city will be tamed by Moore's presence, the wild aggression of stone domesticated by the authority of Moore's imaginative strength:

> For whom the grim museums will behave
> like courteous male bower-birds,
> for whom the agreeable lions lie in wait
> on the steps of the Public Library,

In this visionary utopia of a new "Peaceable Kingdom," stone lions will become lambs "eager to rise and follow through the door up into the reading rooms." For companionship, for activity,

> We can sit down and weep; we can go shopping,
> or play at a game of constantly being wrong
> with a priceless set of vocabularies,
> or we can bravely deplore, but please
> > please come flying.

With the childlike reiteration of the pleading "please," Bishop proffers shared tastes, values, and talents. And yet the lines that follow suggest a more ambivalent if dazzling description of Moore herself:

> With dynasties of negative constructions
> darkening and dying around you,
> with grammar that suddenly turns and shines
> like flocks of sandpipers flying,
> > please come flying.

> Come like a light in the white mackerel sky,
> come like a daytime comet
> with a long unnebulous train of words,
> from Brooklyn, over the Brooklyn Bridge, on this fine morning,
> > please come flying.

83

With their reiterative "come," these closing lines illuminate anticipation. And yet what would it mean to "come" "like a light in the white mackerel sky," a sky already spotted with small, white, fleecy clouds? Would not such a "daytime comet" prove invisible? If Moore's "long unnebulous train of words" spans the journey from Brooklyn to Manhattan, itself bridging the distance between Moore and Bishop, that same "long unnebulous train" clarifies their distance as well. Thus, while invoking Moore's meteoric brilliance, Bishop simultaneously renders that brilliance invisible. In its figural over-reaching and ambiguous constructions invented to express the ambivalence behind what is presented as a genuine desire for reunion, "Invitation to Miss Marianne Moore" reinscribes the differences that inform the Moore-Bishop relationship.[13] How Bishop distinguishes herself from Moore, their rhetorical and philosophical differences, inform the trajectory of Bishop's own poetic development. The direction of that trajectory toward an acknowledgment of loss, as well as the psychoanalytic impulses from which this work on mourning derives, will be the subject of the chapter that follows.

The Memory of Desire and the Landscape of Form: Reading Bishop through Object-Relations Theory

Critics have consistently admired Bishop's accurate eye, the keen powers of observation that surprise the reader into fresh perception. What has been less noted and too frequently neglected is the intense introspection, the deeply inward-looking gaze that makes Bishop's work differ so radically from Moore's. The provisional, deeply ruminative cast of Bishop's poetry lends itself to the subtleties of psychoanalytic criticism, particularly object-relations analysis. That Bishop herself was drawn to Kleinian analysis is, of course, an interesting observation, but more important to the use of object-relations theory in reading Bishop is her concentration on effects of perception, the deeply felt oral emphasis in her work, and the importance of recapturing early childhood experience. If Bishop's relation to poetic influence can be interpreted through a Kleinian understanding of the dynamics of envy and gratitude, Bishop's poems and prose can profitably be read through both Klein and the contemporary, revisionist object-relations theorist, Christopher Bollas.[1] I incorporate Klein and Bollas into my reading of Bishop to suggest not only the powerful instruments provided by analysis for coming to terms with Bishop's poetics, but also to suggest the more generalizable function of object-relations analysis for the reading process.

This chapter presents an object-relations-inflected view of "Crusoe in England" and a brief, Kleinian reading of "In the Village" in order to exemplify the possibilities offered by fusing literary criticism and object-relations analysis. Kleinian analysis is particularly efficacious because of its re-casting of Freudian theory. According to Melanie Klein and her followers, the ego bears within it the traces of the earliest relations of the self with others, the relationship between the infant and her parents. Em-

phasis upon the early mother-infant bond, the nature of that relationship, and the set of issues associated with life at the breast
all establish the importance of a primal scene for Klein that pre-
dates the Oedipal stage and occurs in the first few months of
life. Although nothing may seem further away from the poet's
refined productions, Klein and others argue that all subsequent
interactions and mental processes are governed not only by
inate aptitudes and predilections but are shaped by the formative experiences of the infant as it confronts its environment. My
earlier chapter, "Efforts of Affection," traces the shaping influence of these experiences in the psychodynamics of the
mature relationship of Bishop and her most important female
precursor, Marianne Moore.

Reading Bishop's poetry, however, we may not only deploy
the Kleinian emphases on the good and bad breast, the consequences of maternal deprivation, and the feelings of abandonment that early absence of the "good breast" fosters, we may
look elsewhere within object relations to find an appropriately
responsive field of interpretation. In this regard, the work of
Christopher Bollas seems especially receptive to literary purposes. Crucial to an understanding of Bollas, what marks his
central difference from Freud, is his envisioning the existence of
an unconscious ego knowable to us only through the structures
it creates in fantasies, dreams, and other works of the imagination. This unconscious ego bears within it traces that remain
from the earliest stages of life and are manifest particularly in
dreams. How the self as subject is treated by the dream and how
the shaping unconscious narrates the dream experience reflect
the original ways in which the nascent self was treated by the
combined parental figure. Thus, the structure of the dream, if
read from this point of view, creates the self as subject whose
interactions with its environment recollect the earliest structuring of the ego as mediated through the infant's relationship to
her or his parents. To read the dream as an aesthetic construct
created by the unconscious ego is analogous to our reading a
literary text in order to acquire an understanding of the deep
structures of the imagination that produces the work. Thus, a
distinctly object-relations point of view allows us to intuit the
structures of meaning that invest rhetorical forms. What
emerges is a characteristic paradigm that arrests our attention as

it defines a rubric of associations that remain consistent within a poetic imagination. Although constantly deflected by verbal surprises, this underlying psychodynamics becomes a substructure for the play of tropes as it fashions a rhetoric of stunning multiplicity. In other words, we are not looking here for a single structure so much as for a nexus of associations around which the psyche turns, a pattern of relationality that bespeaks the abiding psychoanalytic themes of Bishop's work and represents it as a coherent whole. I begin therefore with a brief overview of Bollas' insights as they pertain to the interpretation of dreams.

Bollas proposes that we view the dream as an aesthetic act performed by the unconscious ego and that the dream reflects the ego's deep structure: its distinctive, internalized set of object relations. Specifically, Bollas argues that "the person's experience in the dream is based not only on instinctual representations, but on what I believe are ego memories, a view that suggests the ego fulfills a highly idiomatic and creative function when it re-presents these memories in the dream" (Bollas, 64). Bollas asserts that he regards the dream "as a fiction constructed by a unique aesthetic: the transformation of the subject into his thought, specifically, the placing of the self into an allegory of desire and dread that is fashioned by the ego" (Bollas, 64). "From this point of view," Bollas continues, "the dream experience becomes an ironic form of object relation, as the part of the self in the dream is the object of the unconscious ego's articulation of memory and desire. The arrangement of this intrasubjective rendezvous is one of the major accomplishments of the dream experience, an object relation partly contingent on the aesthetic function of the ego" (Bollas, 64).

How might Bollas' conception of the dream and the instruments he offers for its analysis contribute to our understanding of poetics? I suggest that the poem presents a field similar to that of the dream script, and that one can discern within the poem an idiomatic presentation of relations that is analogous to that found through an object-relations analysis of the dream. Whereas a dream interpretation might be built around an understanding of the relationships that inform how the dream subject treats her/his environment, the poem could be comprehended as a verbal field in which the manipulation of tropes, the choices of diction, and perceptual distortions in description all

establish an hallucinatory field that aestheticizes the psychodynamic structures the poem incorporates. Consequently, attention to syntax, diction, and trope can lead us to an understanding of the imagination's underlying structure of object relations.
By reading Elizabeth Bishop's late poem, "Crusoe in England"
through Bollas' theory of dreams, we can approach her work as
an hallucinatory staging of the lineaments of the aestheticizing
ego. Such an analysis leads, therefore, to insights both about the
poem and about the particular structure of consciousness governing the production of the poem. Thus, to read Bishop's
magisterial work in light of Bollas' theory is at once to illuminate the poem and to examine the heuristic efficacy of Bollas's
theory of object relations for a psychoanalytically informed interpretation of poetry.

From its beginning, "Crusoe in England" draws attention to
scenes of naming and birth that reconceptualize the ego's me-
morializing of its origins. By drawing us back to the originary
experiences of conception and nomination, the poem invites associations between the now-to-be memorialized island and the
origins of the individual psyche.

> A new volcano has erupted,
> the papers say, and last week I was reading
> where some ship saw an island being born:
> at first a breath of steam, ten miles away;
> and then a black fleck—basalt, probably—
> rose in the mate's binoculars
> and caught on the horizon like a fly.
> They named it. But my poor old island's still
> un-rediscovered, un-renamable.
> None of the books has ever got it right.

Images of birth and breath govern the identification of this
new island, but Crusoe's island remains "un-rediscovered,"
"unrenamable" because it can be known only by the man
who lived upon it. Crusoe's insistence upon the island's singularity and the difficulties associated with acquiring any knowledge about it whatsoever point toward the highly private
character of the place and speak to the task of the poem, a
description of this intimate and estranged landscape. Crusoe's

perception of the singular aspect of this island demands from him an interpretation of experience that depends solely upon himself.

Crusoe begins his description of the island by emphasizing possession, envisioning geography as something he owns:

> Well, I had fifty-two
> miserable, small volcanoes I could climb
> with a few slithery strides—

The description of the island's volcanoes contains several characteristics of Crusoe's epistemological procedures. First, he counts the volcanoes; secondly, the number he identifies is coincidentally the number of weeks in the year; thirdly, the volcanoes appear miniaturized (there is a radical disruption of perspective); and, finally, the volcanoes are envisioned through anthropomorphic associations: "naked and leaden, with their heads blown off." By stating that there are fifty-two volcanoes, Crusoe invites a metaphysical synaesthesia that recurs throughout the poem. The "coincidence" of the number invites us to think of the volcanoes not only as physical phenomena but as objects that demarcate temporal divisions as well. Similarly, the volcanoes partake of another mode of being as they assume the attributes of animistic beings who are "naked" and whose "heads are blown off." These volcanic eruptions are the first in a series of occasions throughout the poem where the effects of violence shatter as they merge with anomalous human forms. This anthropomorphic troping is followed by the surreal perception that the volcanoes are miniaturized, and that to account for such a perception, Crusoe must have become a "giant," in which case

> I couldn't bear to think what size
> the goats and turtles were,
> or the gulls, or the overlapping rollers

As elsewhere in the poem, here the consequences of perception cause Crusoe a sharp revulsion. This diminution that masks the threat of giantism is the first in a series of perspectival shifts that participate in the creation of a vertiginous landscape. In trying to "make sense of" the phenomena he observes, Crusoe only deepens his feelings of discomfort, therefore participating in the creation of an horrific sense of place marked by outsized forms and apparently inexplicable phenomena. Repetition combines with perspectival disruption to create a claustrophobic sense of space:

> —a glittering hexagon of rollers
> closing and closing in, but never quite,
> glittering and glittering, though the sky
> was mostly overcast.

The anti-natural "glittering" that reflects nothing present contributes to the island's uncanny quality. Speculating on the weather, Crusoe envisions the island as a "sort of cloud-dump":

> ... All the hemisphere's
> left-over clouds arrived and hung
> above the craters—their parched throats
> were hot to touch.

The left-over clouds fail to shed rain on the craters' parched throats, whose thirst remains unslaked. Like the earlier description of the volcanoes' heads that are blown off, here the craters' "parched throats" recall anthropomorphism combined with suffering. Orality predominates as the craters fail to receive any succor from the clouds as earlier the rollers received no sun to account for their "glitter." In the logic of object relations, these tropes suggest that the self, in trying to make sense of this revulsive landscape, conceptualizes its geography in human terms that are marked by violence, a failure of reciprocity, and lack of satisfaction. The sun and its reflection, rain and the parched throats, relationships that should be reciprocal, are not; consequently, geography is mediated by the failure of the environment to fill the landscape's needs. This is an externalization of a pattern that emerges throughout the poem, where oral needs are met with violence, attempts to make sense of the incomprehensible render only further confusion, and the possibility of relief results in an extenuation of suffering. Though it "rains so much," that rain does nothing to relieve the heat generated on the island. In a graphic description of the consolations of the domestic turned horrific, Crusoe asks,

> And why sometimes the whole place hissed?
> The turtles lumbered by, high-domed,
> hissing like teakettles.
> (And I'd have given years, or taken a few,
> for any sort of kettle, of course.)
> The folds of lava, running out to sea,
> would hiss. I'd turn. And then they'd prove
> to be more turtles.

Oppressive replication possesses this land as it will continue to do. Possession breeds excess:

> And I had waterspouts. Oh,
> half a dozen at a time, far out,
> they'd come and go, advancing and retreating,
> their heads in cloud, their feet in moving patches
> of scuffed-up white.

These "sacerdotal beings of glass" have heads and feet; they, too, resemble outsized, grotesque human forms. If the geographic is perceived through the human, the animal can be confused with the geological in this animated world where resemblances among categories continuously occur (even the water that spirals up in these "glass chimneys" resembles smoke). Closing the first movement of the poem, a description of the geological and climatic conditions expressed through images of oral deprivation, Crusoe comments that the glass chimneys were "beautiful, yes, but not much company."

Sitting upon the edge of a crater, Crusoe contemplates the advantages of self-pity in a desire to attach some sort of explanation to his being where he is. His hope is that by adapting to the place, by finding some sort of accommodation with it, he will feel "at home." The issue of being "at home" remains vital as Crusoe variously tries to account for the stunning singularity of the island, the stunted character of the vegetation, and the severe limitations it imposes upon the possibilities for variation. In his attempts to adjust to such a landscape of privation, Crusoe seeks to alter his own state of consciousness by making a "home-brew." This attempt at intoxication becomes a bizarre kind of Dionysiac celebration as Crusoe plays his "home-made flute . . . and "whoop(s)" and "dance(s) . . . among the goats."

If such self-created celebrations provide a brief respite from the overwhelming sameness of the island and its isolation, a more extended philosophical consolation cannot be found.

> Because I didn't know enough.
> Why didn't I know enough of something?
> Greek drama or astronomy? The books
> I'd read were full of blanks;
> the poems—well, I tried
> reciting to my iris-beds,
> "They flash upon that inward eye,
> which is the bliss . . ." The bliss of what?
> One of the first things that I did
> when I got back was look it up.

If the clouds fail to provide relief, if nature does not proffer consolation, so the literary, the world of print, cannot accommodate this kind of loneliness. The bliss of solitude remains outside the ken of memory because it is not replicated in experience.

Aversiveness continues as the noises of sheep and goats echo in Crusoe's ears, causing him pain. In an attempt to achieve a respite from the "questioning shrieks, the equivocal replies/over a ground of hissing rain/ and hissing, ambulating turtles," Crusoe again tries the transformative powers of the imagination.

> When all the gulls flew up at once, they sounded
> like a big tree in a strong wind, its leaves.
> I'd shut my eyes and think about a tree,
> an oak, say, with real shade, somewhere.

This internalized vision occurs without comment, apparently providing no real relief. In an intensified attempt to achieve some kind of companionship, Crusoe would grab a billy-goat's beard and "look at him." Reciprocity is, however, denied as this forced gesture of communication is met by defence:

> His pupils, horizontal, narrowed up
> and expressed nothing, or a little malice.

Like the man-moth, who, when stared at, "stares back and

closes up his eye," the goat refuses contact. To break the bore-
dom, Crusoe tries dying a baby goat "bright red," "and then his
mother wouldn't recognize him." This scene of the mother who
will not recognize her baby is but a further extenuation of what
by now forms a pattern in the poem wherein one element of a
pair fails the other, where reciprocity is rejected or deferred.
This deferral of recognition becomes more violent in Crusoe's
dreams, for, if the descriptions of the land are marked by tropes
that speak to the animistic orality of the island, the dream-
fantasy reveals a structuring of experience in which disappointment leads to violence (recall the trace of violence in the blown-
off heads of the volcanoes).

Instead of the mother goat being unable to recognize her offspring, now it is Crusoe who dreams of "slitting a baby's throat,
mistaking it/ for a baby goat." Generation, whether of islands,
polliwogs, or human beings becomes a subject for meditation as
Crusoe's nightmare vision appears.

> . . . I'd have
> nightmares of other islands
> stretching away from mine, infinities
> of islands, islands spawning islands,
> like frogs' eggs turning into polliwogs
> of islands, knowing that I had to live
> on each and every one, eventually,
> for ages, registering their flora,
> their fauna, their geography.

The explicit frame of the nightmare governs this fantasy which
reveals objects that make a claim on the individual, a claim that
is based on the need to register, to record the endlessly proliferating islands' facts. Regeneration here is asexual, devoid of any
notion of union with an other; instead, it conveys a sense of endlessly demanding duplication that fails to result in companionship or the acknowledgment of difference. The burden of such a
vision is broken only by Friday's appearance. Friday provides
the friendship Crusoe has craved. Moreover, unlike Crusoe's,
Friday's relationship with the other natural beings is compan-
ionable: "He'd pet the baby goats sometimes,/ and race with
them, or carry one around." Crusoe views him with admiration:
"—Pretty to watch; he had a pretty body."

After Crusoe is rescued and returns to England, objects formerly endowed with life are no longer invested with meaning. Without a purpose, they are rendered uninteresting. Life is bestowed upon an object through use; observation stems from need.

> The knife there on the shelf—
> it reeked of meaning, like a crucifix.
> It lived. How many years did I
> beg it, implore it, not to break?
> I knew each nick and scratch by heart,
> the bluish blade, the broken tip,
> the lines of wood-grain on the handle . . .
> Now it won't look at me at all.
> The living soul has dribbled away.
> My eyes rest on it and pass on.

The reciprocity of interest born of necessity has died. Objects are devalued because they have left their landscape of use and are now merely a legacy of past experience. If mutual interest is initiated by Crusoe's need, then rejection by the object—"it won't look at me at all"—results from the object's being released from relationship by the perceiver, released from its importance as a tool for survival.

If, throughout the poem, it has remained up to Crusoe to make sense of his world, he has done so through failed attempts at logic, rationalization, word play and related equivocations (Mont d'Espoir/ Mount Despair). Repeatedly, the structures of Crusoe's unconscious have revealed to him a world of striking insufficiency, sameness, and lack of reciprocity. The unconscious ego has predicated a geography of otherness based upon replication in which needs fail to be met, desires are vanquished, isolation is the norm. What challenges this view is the appearance of Friday, and it is Friday who outlasts all other objects. Unlike geography, fauna, flora, or the instruments of human use, Friday survives intact; his memory infused with affection and meaningfulness. The locution "—And Friday, my dear Friday, died of measles/seventeen years ago come March," with its plangent echo of Friday's name and the implacable momentum of "come," assures the continued significance of the ties of affection shared with Crusoe.

If we read "Crusoe in England" as a fantasy structured by the unconscious ego that replicates the earliest object relations, the poem yields nothing less than the history of the authorial imagination described as an isolated self faced with lack of reciprocity, unmet needs, and the frustration of misrecognition that breeds a murderous anger. In the face of such a world, the imagination responds with music, art, and fragmented memories to find requisite tools for survival. The failures and successes of these attempts transcribe the earliest object relations, for how a mind treats the world reflects how the mother/father treated the self in infancy. Human connection alone redeems and restores a life of intense loneliness. A world of insufficiency acquires meaning through the beloved appearance of Friday, the appearance of one now lost. The poem achieves this elegiac recognition as it moves beyond the privation of the earliest object relations (herein depicted by the aridity of geography) to address instead a grammar of desire that sustains the mutuality of human affection over and beyond the confines of death.

This desire for the mutuality of human affection underlies the psychodynamics of Bishop's story, "In the Village," where early experience is rendered in vividly sensuous terms. Bishop's emphasis on perceptions in this story leads the reader into the experiential responses of Bishop as a child who witnesses her mother's failed attempts to come out of mourning and resume her life. The child's reactions to her mother's behavior mark a fundamental moment in the young girl's experience, for it determines the forms that compensation, defense, and sublimation will assume throughout Bishop's career. In order to read "In the Village" as a story of aesthetic initiation, it is advantageous to trace its development through psychoanalytic theory, particularly those ideas that Klein associates with early infantile anxiety situations and the individual's responses to the process of mourning.

Klein argues that for the girl the most profound anxiety is associated with her fear that she will irreparably harm her mother. "The little girl has a sadistic desire, originating in the early stages of the Oedipus conflict, to rob the mother's body of its contents, namely, the father's penis, faeces, children, and to destroy the mother herself. This desire gives rise to anxiety lest the mother should in her turn rob the little girl herself of the contents of her body (especially of children) and lest her body should be destroyed or mutilated." "In my view," Klein continues, "this anxiety, which I have found in the analyses of girls and women to be the deepest anxiety of all, represents the little girl's earliest danger situation. I have come to realize that the dread of being alone, of the loss of love, and of the love object, which Freud holds to be the basic infantile danger situation in girls, is a modification of the anxiety situation I have just described."[2] Bishop, in her story, shows us a girl reacting to an already injured mother in mourning, someone who articulates through her scream the extent of her inner wounds. The child therefore must confront not only the inevitable fear that she will damage the mother; she must also face the reality of an already damaged mother from whom she has been and will again be separated. Thus the child's anxieties would be intensified by the objective reality of her mother's condition and the tenuousness of her presence. Threat of loss of the mother is a secondary fear that Klein recognizes as arising from the child's need to prove to herself that the mother has not been damaged:

> I have come to realize that the dread of being alone, of the loss of love, and of the love object, which Freud holds to be the basic infantile danger situation in girls, is a modification of the anxiety situation I have just described. When the little girl who fears the mother's assault upon her body cannot *see* her mother, it intensifies the anxiety. The presence of the real, loving mother diminishes the dread of the terrifying mother, whose image is introjected into the child's mind. At a later stage of development the content of the dread changes from that of an attacking mother to the dread that the real, loving mother may be lost and that the girl will be left solitary and forsaken. (Klein, 92–93)

In her attempt to assuage these fears, the girl wishes to make reparation, to restore to the mother her strength. She may do this as the painter, Ruth Kjar, does in Klein's "Infantile Anxiety Situations," by the painting of portraits, or such restitution can come about through the creation of a story.

"In the Village" provides such an attempt at reparation, but an attempt that is cognizant of and does not violate the conditions surrounding the mother's mental deterioration and subsequent absence. Rather, reparation is made by the introduction of alternative sources of life-affirming power, the presence of the blacksmith, Nate, and the solace of nature. "In the Village" may be read, then, not only as a story about a woman's attempt to come out of mourning, but as a description of a child's process of mourning, of her attempts to accommodate her mother's disappearance and keep her world intact. What counters the mother's shattering scream must be a sound of equal power, the clang of Nate's hammer. But it is not the clang alone that silences the mother's scream; rather it is the masculine powers of the smithy as they are submerged in nature, in the "slp" of the river that flows over the "old sunken fender of Malcolm McNeil's Ford."[3] We will return to this moment when we reach the end of the story; first we need to observe the ways the narrative accumulates its disparate impressions of the grieving, unstable mother and those people and objects in the world that give the child pleasure. "In the Village" opens with the sound of the mother's scream, a scream that permeates and lingers in the atmosphere of the village, of home.[4]

> A scream, the echo of a scream, hangs over that Nova Scotian village. No one hears it; it hangs there forever, a slight stain in those pure blue skies, skies that travelers compare to those of Switzerland, too dark, too blue, so that they seem to keep on darkening a little more around the horizon—or is it around the rims of the eyes?—the color of the cloud of bloom on the elm trees, the violet on the fields of oats; something darkening over the woods and waters as well as the sky. The scream hangs like that, unheard, in memory—in the past, in the present, and those years between. It was not even loud to begin with, perhaps. It just came there to live, forever—not loud, just alive forever. Its pitch would be the pitch of my village. Flick the lightning rod on top of the church steeple with your fingernail and you will hear it." (Bishop, 251)

The stain of the scream is ineradicable; it is always present, sustained by the lightning rod, outpost of village danger.

The first scene, of the mother's being fitted for a purple dress that would announce her coming out of mourning, contains a description of a pattern of return, absence, and return, expressed through the detached tones of third-person narration.

First, she had come home, with her child. Then she had gone away again, alone, and left the child. Then she had come home. Then she had gone away again, with her sister; and now she was home again.

"Unaccustomed to having her back, the child stood now in the doorway, watching" (Bishop, 252). What the child observes is a scene of loss, incipient danger, and tension all expressed by the figure of the dressmaker who "was crawling around and around on her knees eating pins as Nebuchadnezzar had crawled eating grass" (Bishop, 252). This image of the mad Biblical king's eating grass is the first of a sequence of oral images of ingestion, where objects, sometimes dangerous, are placed in the mouth and swallowed. Ingestion of objects suggests the narrator's attempts to incorporate external experience into herself. The five-cent piece that the child will later swallow, becomes, she imagines, a part of her, as the rice grains in the china teacup leave a trace in the substance they touch. If ingestion functions throughout the story as a symbol of psychic incorporation, so elimination is of equal importance, symbolizing the expulsion of negative or bad feelings. Viewing the idyllic, homelike scene at the blacksmith's shop, the narrator observes a horse being fitted:

> The horse is the real guest, however. . . . Manure piles up behind him, suddenly, neatly. He, too, is very much at home. He is enormous. His rump is like a brown, glossy globe of the whole brown world. His ears are secret entrances to the underworld. His nose is supposed to feel like velvet and does, with ink spots under milk all over its pink. (Bishop, 257)

The brown, rounded shape of the rump and the "secret entrances" of the ears convey the excremental and anal images beyond the piles of manure to the horse himself. Similarly, Nelly the cow's excrement gains the narrator's attention.

> Nelly, oblivious, makes cow flops. Smack. Smack. Smack. Smack. It is fascinating. I cannot take my eyes off her. Then I step around them: fine dark-green and lacy and watery at the edges. (Bishop, 263)

Excrement and the process of elimination acquire a benignant power that functions as part of the process of mourning. Klein writes, "Just as the young child passing through the depressive position is struggling, in his unconscious mind, with the task of establishing and integrating his inner world, so the mourner goes through the pain of re-establishing and re-integrating it."[5]

Mourning, its efficacy and its limitations, is the subject of "In the Village,"and it is the child's mourning for both parents that is the story's concern. Developments of the mourning process are crucial both on their symbolic and literal levels. Klein notes that for the mourner tears act to expel feeling. She suggests that "through tears, which in the unconscious mind are equated to excrement, the mourner not only expresses his feelings and thus eases tension, but also expels his 'bad' feelings and his 'bad' objects, and this adds to the relief obtained through crying."[6] The child's fascination with the horse's and cow's excrement in "In the Village" may be related to similar unconscious feelings (the emphasis on excrement signifies the release of "bad" feelings). Part of the drama of the child's process of recovery (or partial recovery) in Bishop's story is contained within the economy of ingestion and elimination, the taking in and expulsion of good and bad objects until a viable sum of positive objects allows the self to be sustained and to grow. Not only the horse and the cow, but nature in its entirety shows the way towards establishing the good object and ridding oneself of the overwhelming effects of the bad. In this regard, Klein notes that "the poet tells us that 'Nature mourns with the mourner.' " She continues, "I believe that 'Nature' in this connection represents the internal good mother. This experience of mutual sorrow and sympathy in internal relationships, however, is again bound up with external ones."[7] Elimination is just one way that the bad object is controlled by nature. If nature as the good mother can come to substitute for, not simply represent, the internal good mother, then it presents an alternative space in which the work of mourning can be accomplished. Because she must do without the validating presence of the external good mother, the child seeks elsewhere, in nature, for the qualities originally associated with maternal nurturance. The world of the female is surrounded by danger, not only the danger surrounding the unreliable mother but that of the figure of the allegorically named Miss Gurley, the seamstress, as well, who, in a portrait of fairytale-like magical

99

surrealism, is described as a mythical figure of mysterious, potentially malevolent power.

> Her house is littered with scraps of cloth and tissue-paper patterns, yellow, pinked, with holes in the shapes of A, B, C, and D in them, and numbers; and threads everywhere like a fine vegetation. She has a bosom full of needles with threads ready to pull out and make nests with. She sleeps in her thimble. A gray kitten once lay on the treadle of her sewing machine, where she rocked it as she sewed, like a baby in a cradle, but it got hanged on the belt. Or did she make that up? But another gray-and-white one lies now by the arm of the machine, in imminent danger of being sewn into a turban." (Bishop, 258)

Entanglement and infanticide are to be feared in such a place. As in "Crusoe in England," when Crusoe dreams of mistaking a human baby for a baby goat, here the kitten is compared to "a baby in a cradle" just before it gets hanged. The "bosom full of needles," image of rejecting maternity, combines with the magical properties associated with Miss Gurley as femininity attains the attributes of danger and power.

Opposed to these associations, the masculine world of the blacksmith's shop is a place of security and wonder:

> Oh, beautiful sounds, from the blacksmith's shop at the end of the garden! Its gray roof, with patches of moss, could be seen above the lilac bushes. Nate was there—Nate, wearing a long black leather apron over his trousers and bare chest, sweating hard, a black leather cap on top of dry, thick, black-and-gray curls, a black sooty face; iron filings, whiskers, and gold teeth, all together, and a smell of red-hot metal and horses' hoofs.
> *Clang.*
> The pure note: pure and angelic. (Bishop, 252–253)

Here things can happen instantly; wishes are immediately fulfilled:

> "Make me a ring! Make me a ring, Nate!" Instantly it is made; it is mine. (Bishop, 257)

Overwhelming as the repercussions of her mother's scream may be ("The dress was all wrong. She screamed./ The child vanishes") Nate's blacksmith shop at the end of the garden offers another place where the child, through sublimating her desires for her mother, can learn of the saving possibilities of the external world. The "good enough mother" is created in this masculine/natural space. Seeking decisiveness and certainty, the child discovers these qualities in the world of Nate, the blacksmith. Security and a sense of being "at home" are associated with the shop. But the human province alone does not suffice to preserve positive feelings indefinitely. Instead, the child imagines a merger of the blacksmith's with the natural world. Against the background of human trauma, nature offers the solace of peace.

The story's climactic event of the fire at a neighbor's barn (with the concomitant fear that the noise and light will upset the child's mother) is conveyed both vividly and at a certain remove. There is a dissociation between the precipitating events and their effect upon the child. In retrospect, the narrator, who now writes in the first person, must guess her earlier responses: "But one night, in the middle of the night, there is a fire. The church bell wakes me up. It is in the room with me; red flames are burning the wallpaper beside the bed. I suppose I shriek" (Bishop, 268). Here the illusion that the child's room is burning is presented as fact while her response to this misperception is presented as surmise. So, at the scene's end, the narrator, reflecting on the close of the tumultuous night, records, "I suppose I go to sleep" (Bishop, 270). Such suppositions are in stark contrast to the vividness with which the circumstances that surround these purported responses are portrayed. The fragmentary recollection of events announces gaps in memory, perhaps a result of severe repression. The absence of the mother is presented through circumlocution: "Now the front bedroom is empty. My older aunt has gone back to Boston and my other aunt is making plans to go there after a while, too" (Bishop, 271). No mention of the mother is made, as the trauma of her departure is controlled through such dissociative expression. Yet the mother is not altogether silenced. Her presence is manifested in the packages the grandmother sends and that the child carries to the post office. The child's first loyalty is to her mother, a fact made clear when she pretends not to hear Nate when he calls to her on her way to take the packages to the post office.

101

In the story's final scene, the child, carrying her package, stops on the bridge and stares down "into the river." What she sees is the culmination of her powers of sublimation, the view into a natural world that includes but does not destroy the "man-made" artifact. The vision of the submerged fender of Malcolm McNeil's Ford which is "supposed to be a disgrace to us all," offers the child an ideal object, one that is static but surrounded by movement, an object that is manufactured but altered by the natural environment it inhabits.

> From above, the trout look as transparent as the water, but if one did catch a fish, it would be opaque enough, with a little slick moon-white belly with a pair of tiny, pleated, rose-pink fins on it. The leaning willows soak their narrow yellowed leaves.
> Clang.
> *Clang.*
> Nate is shaping a horseshoe.
> Oh, beautiful pure sound!
> It turns everything else to silence.
> But still, once in a while, the river gives an unexpected gurgle. "Slp," it says out of glassy-ridged brown knots sliding along the surface. (Bishop, 273–274)

While the narrator initially suggests that Nate's sound turns everything to silence, other sounds do intrude— not only the sound of the river, the "slp," but the stain of the scream that in the story's opening leaves its trace in the sky. But with the combined sounds of the clang and the river, "Now there is no scream." "Once there was one and it settled slowly down to earth one hot summer afternoon; or did it float up, into that dark, too dark, blue sky? But surely it has gone away, forever." The phrase that casts the scream into oblivion simultaneously restores it, for "but surely" raises a doubt, a doubt that is followed by the reverberations of what seems to be the scream cast out into the world:

> It sounds like a bell buoy out at sea.
> It is the elements speaking: earth, air, fire, water. But the "it," which grammatically appears to refer to the scream, contextually refers not to the scream but to the clang (the ambiguity of the pronoun renders both meanings possible).

It sounds like a bell buoy out at sea.

It is the elements speaking: earth, air, fire, water.

All those other things—clothes, crumbling postcards, broken china; things damaged and lost, sickened or destroyed; even the frail almost-lost scream—are they too frail for us to hear their voices long, too mortal?

Nate!

Oh, beautiful sound, strike again!" (Bishop, 274)

Clothes, postcards, china have all revealed their vulnerability to time and lead, synechdochically, to the almost-lost scream. What provides permanence in this world of fragile mortality is the assurance of Nate's power, which the narrator calls to "strike again." But the desire to hear Nate's clang is not felt in isolation. Rather it is a sound that is dispersed into and through the natural world. Nature provides the fluidity, the movement, the sense of process that absorbs the clang and makes it part of its world.

"In the Village" can be understood as the reparative expression of the adult self reflecting upon the initial loss of both parents and the tenuous aspects of that most important of human relationships, the mother-infant bond. The child in the story (who moves from the third person "she" to the first) witnesses the loss of things in this world, be they relationships, individuals, or objects. Against the instability of the first relationship, the recurrent maternal absences, and the perception of an insecure relationship with the wounded mother, the child discovers an alternative possibility, one marked by assurance and security, an alternative that is not simply the blacksmith's, a world identified with masculinity and craftsmanship, *but the displacement of craft into the natural world which lends a mutability that changes but does not destroy.* It is this vision of the saving artifact, of the object in nature, that the fender of McNeil's Ford represents. For it is both sounds, the clang and the "slp" of the river that combine to create the silencing of the scream. What offers reparation to the mourning child in the adult of this story is a vision of masculine performance that is invested in the natural world. Nature substitutes for the female; instead of the trauma of madness, it offers the calm modulations of process. Finally, "In the Village" may be read as a working through of the process of mourning itself. By the story's end, the scream has vanished, but only provisionally vanished, for, if we recall the opening passage, the scream leaves its stain on all future remembrance. Bishop's attention to objects throughout the story, her focus on disparate physical phenomena, points to processes of ingestion, elimination, and incorporation as the imagination works to accommodate its grief and overcome mourning. From the primary anxiety situation of confronting the abandoning mother, the narrator moves toward a reinvestment of feeling and recognition of her mother's absence by seeking assurance in an alternative medium. Throughout her work, Bishop will re-create the power of craft and attest to the salvific mutability of nature in order to redress feelings of abandonment and loss. "In the Village" speaks to the origins of that aesthetic and philosophical choice. Through a Kleinian reading of the story, one may view the structure of an imagination that reveals loss converted into strength. The mourning process is successfully worked through as the narrator finds in the act of sublimation an alternative resource for her affections. Abandoned by the mother, she turns to the world of the male and to the realm of the natural as the source for feeling. And it is here, in this alternative home, that Bishop finds the fluid permanence she so desires.

If "In the Village" sketches a psychically successful journey from mourning to reparation, "Crusoe in England" delineates a similar trajectory with a more somber outcome. Like "In the Village," "Crusoe in England" describes a site of loss, but here invention, while it can temporarily stave off loneliness, cannot survive the return home. What constitutes the difference between the losses suffered in the story and poem is that Bishop, while she can constitute a world of meanings where human craft conspires with nature to create a safe haven for art, cannot constitute a world of sustained human relationships. Friday's loss proves irreparable because in this poem of unreconciled mourning, no other object comes to take his place. The haunting singularity that marks Crusoe's island speaks to Friday's reality as well, for he can neither be forgotten nor replaced. Reparation here would mean the internalization of Friday into the self and substitution for him in the external world. But neither internalization nor substitution occurs; instead Crusoe is left at home with loss. That "In the Village" should represent a more successful mourning process, that here reparation should discover itself in art, reveals the efficacy of Bishop's transformation of feelings from the lost mother to the regenerative father, from the world of women to the craft of men. The scream, if it is stilled, loses its power, as I have suggested, through the force of an alternative collaboration of male-identified reality and the natural sphere. Whereas the narrator in "Crusoe in England" assumes a male persona, that of Crusoe himself, and while what is mourned is therefore a homoerotic relationship, the masculinized provenance does not save the loss from being irreparable. What remains with Crusoe is the fact of Friday's death which echoes with all the plangency of sorrow. On the other hand, what both "Crusoe in England" and "In the Village" attest to is the importance of the process of mourning for Bishop. Our sense of ourselves and of the world comes, object-relations theorists would argue, from that earliest originary relationship of the infant-mother dyad. If, as in Bishop's case, that relationship is marked by disruption and abandonment, is it any wonder that all the inventiveness in Crusoe's possession cannot redress his subsequent loss? If the power of art to find reparation through mourning exists in Bishop, it may be found in the merger of a male-identified craft and attentiveness to the external world, for it is here, amidst the assurance of such an alternative place, that Bishop discovers the power that mitigates grief.

Object Relations, Influence, and the Woman Poet

W HY OBJECT relations? It has been my contention that this revisionary psychoanalytic model offers a particularly advantageous method for reading poetry.[1] Specifically, I argue that reading Bishop through object-relations theory yields a number of insights; foremost among them, an understanding of the psychodynamics of literary influence relations as they work themselves out between Bishop and her most formidable predecessor, Marianne Moore. In addition to the individual insights provided through such an approach, one can discern a larger, revisionist conceptualization of poetic influence through the lens of object relations. Particularly, one can understand the workings of influence not in the agonistic mode of Freudian theory but through the dynamics of gift exchange, the feelings of envy and gratitude that emerge from the originary primal scene, and the infant's nursing at her mother's breast. The conflictual responses that result from this experience—fear that the mother may prove insufficient, pleasure when a reciprocal balance of supply and demand has been reached, anxiety that the breast may be robbed of sufficient resources, bemusement at the site of the feeding and the rejecting breast—all can be transposed to the modulations of literary creativity and the interrelationship between the poet and her literary predecessor.

But a reading of aesthetics through object relations itself can be understood as returning to a fundamental question: "What do we look for, what do we hope for, when we read literature?" Here the current work of Christopher Bollas brings object relations in contact with aesthetic theory. Bollas asserts that the aesthetic moment itself is a "caesura in time when the subject feels held in symmetry and solitude by the spirit of the object" (Bollas, 31). If that object is a poem and the subject the reader, then the question becomes, "What is it specifically about this poem that creates the effect of time stopping, the feeling the reader experiences of being held by the poem, and the recognition that one is undergoing an aesthetic moment: What is it about this particular text that leads to a rapport with the sacred object?" To examine how this sense of rapport is created we need to return again to the original scene of instruction, the infant at the mother's breast, for it is here, Bollas argues, that the formative process that will henceforth be decisive in our choice of the aesthetic moment occurs. Bollas writes,

> The mother's idiom of care and the infant's experience of this handling is one of the first if not the earliest human aesthetic. It is the most profound occasion when the nature of the self is formed and transformed by the environment. The uncanny pleasure of being held by a poem, a composition, a painting, or, for that matter, any object, rests on those moments when the infant's internal world is partly given form by the mother since he cannot shape them or link them together without her coverage." (Bollas, 32)

Bollas describes the mother's facilitating presence as one that is not recognized as distinct by the child, but is rather perceived as a transformational process without a specific, individuated agent. This "transformational" moment from a state of distress to the alleviation of conflict, anxiety, or discomfort is what the later psyche seeks in the aesthetic realm. Consequently, according to Bollas,

> This first human aesthetic informs the development of personal character (which is the utterance of self through the manner of being rather than the representation of the mind) and will predispose all future aesthetic experiences that place the person in subjective rapport with an object ... each aesthetic experience is transformational. ... The transformational object seems to promise the beseeching subject an experience where self fragmentations will be integrated through a processing form. (Bollas, 33)

Attention to the primary scene of relating therefore illuminates the cast of the individual artist's as well as the reader's subsequent aesthetic moments. The "first human aesthetic" affects all future moments, and thus reading texts with an eye for the psychodynamics of object relations reveals not only the informing paradigm of the infant's relation to the mother, but the aesthetic implications of the infant's first reciprocal relationship. The mother creates for her infant a holding environment, and it is this environment that creates an "idiom of care" which, according to Bollas, is "one of the first if not the earliest human aesthetic" (Bollas, 32). What characterizes this idiom of care influences all future aesthetic and interpersonal moments on the part of the developing individual. The artist, therefore, reflects in her future works the initial "idiom of care" first proffered by the mother.

In addition to reflecting the mother's idiom of care, the writer presents a reparative idiom that attempts to compensate for the mother's perceived inadequacies. Thus, a text such as "Crusoe in England" can be understood as the delineation of an insufficient holding environment and the narrator's attempts to create his own idiom of care against a background of wondrous depletion. Indeed, the compensatory nature of object-relations aesthetics gestures towards a fundamental theory of art: namely, that creativity springs from the desire to make reparation to the limited mother, to return to the holding environment reconceived by the daughter-poet, an environment that through its reformulation attempts to make up the deficit of the original, infantile relation. The terms that operate here are envy and gratitude, need and satiety, and Klein's observations regarding these primary, shaping forces can be used to illuminate aspects of the psychodynamics of literary creativity as they work themselves out in the mature writer.

Consequently, my foregoing discussion of Bishop's "Efforts of Affection" investigates the forces of envy and gratitude that operate in the daughter-poet's psyche as it traces the rhetorical strategies Bishop evokes to negotiate her way between the potentially destructive power of envy and the rehabilitative force of gratitude. The bemusement Bishop experiences when she meditates on Moore is itself useful, Klein would argue, for it allows Bishop the space afforded by *misrecognition*, thus enabling Bishop to survive the ambiguous double binds of a mother who simultaneously gives and withholds.

If envy and gratitude are the primary, polar emotions that dominate the originary site of poetic influence, then related feelings of loss, mourning, and reparation govern literary productivity itself. At the heart of Bishop's work lies a desire to make restitution, to find a compensatory gift that will make up to the

wounded, abandoning mother all that her daughter has paradoxically lost. The desire to make reparations stems from the
interior need to replenish the self, to find a way to survive the
first and most crucial loss, that of the mother. Any writer's work
may thus be read as the product of the desire to make reparation. Interestingly, Bishop makes this search for reparation itself
the *theme* of much of her strongest work as she delineates the
longing that finds its origins in her sense of loss. Most power-
fully, "In the Village" describes a process of mourning wherein
the loss of the psychically wounded mother is compensated
for by the re-creation of pleasure in the world of masculine-
identified creativity submerged in nature. This compensatory
formulation seeks to excise the bitter disappointments of maternal, erratic behavior and replace them with a steadfast, immediately rewarding artistic production that survives the ravages of
time. This reconceptualization of the benign provenance of art
allows Bishop to create an alternative home that, if it does not
silence the mother's scream, allows it to fade and be replaced by
a more immediate and enduring craft. Thus, Bishop constructs
an accommodation between the intermittent occasions of artistic
production and the inherent mutability of nature. Loss and
abrupt departure are re-cast once artistic production is embed-
ded in a natural sphere of temporality that allows both for departure and return. Such acceptance of temporality affords
the occasion for acceptance of loss as the possibility for reparation remains alive in the natural world. Thus, gratitude, envy,
mourning, and reparation, the fundamental feelings that dominate the object-relations-inflected psyche can be understood
as informing Bishop's aesthetics both in the sphere of poetic
influence and in the creation of her individuating artistic resolu-
tions. Object relations allows us, therefore, to consider the trajectory of Bishop's aesthetic commitments while enabling us to
read her work with an attentiveness to the deep structure and
governing origins of her imagination.

Object relations, however, offers us more. By investigating the
interpsychic processes that govern a writer and her precursor,
we can begin to decipher patterns that illuminate our own experience as readers. For all of us, as readers, are affected by the
formative process of life at the mother's breast. The individuating psychodynamics of one reader-writer's (in this case,

Bishop's) relation to her parent and her parental texts affords us access to the processes that inform reading relationships more generally. If we understand reading as a process of reparation, a revisionist procedure of re-making what we read, then analysis of that process of revision enables us more accurately to assess the distinctive psychic life of any individual reader. Reading Bishop reading Moore, therefore, enables us to pinpoint more precisely than heretofore not simply Moore's and Bishop's mutual poetic origins, but the specific turns that differentiate Bishop from Moore, thereby shedding light on the distinctive workings of Bishop's *intrapsychic* life.

Finally, reading Bishop through Moore enables us to trace an alternative paradigm to male, modernist tradition, a paradigm based upon a female-centered model for literary influence that traces the processes of influence relations in terms of the pre-Oedipal stage, thereby acknowledging the primary importance of the mother and hence the literary foremother. That the relationship between a daughter-poet and her literary foremother contains within it the increased complication of the younger poet's desire to emulate and revise a writer already marginalized by tradition adds to the difficulties of the process and accentuates the need to make reparation to the already decentered poetic mother. How the dynamics of this female-inflected theory of influence relations swerves from the male model is a concern that governs not only a discussion of Bishop's relation to Moore but all influence relations between and among women. The development of an alternative tradition of what might be defined as a female-inflected modernism can be understood as commencing with the recognition of the difference gender makes in accounting for one's relation to the dominant tradition. Object relations offers to this reconstitution of a female-centered tradition the possibility of an heuristic theory that finds its origins in the mother-infant relationship and locates the psychodynamics that inform every future artistic production in the initial scene of the infant at the mother's breast. How the daughter-poet learns to express her own word, how she comes to differentiate herself from her mother while dealing with her own feelings of aggression, loss, and anxiety is the story that an object-relations-inflected reading of art attempts to tell. The implications of this story are just beginning to unfold.

❖ *Notes* ❖

INTRODUCTION

1. Gilbert and Gubar, *No Man's Land: The Place of the Woman Writer in the Twentieth Century. Volume 1: The War of the Words* (New Haven: Yale University Press, 1987), 200. All future references to this work will appear in parentheses within the text.

2. Sigmund Freud, *Complete Psychological Works* (London: Hogarth Press and the Institute of Psychoanalysis, 1953–74), vol. 3, 139.

CHAPTER ONE

1. All references to Elizabeth Bishop's memoir, "Efforts of Affection: A Memoir of Marianne Moore" will be followed by page numbers in parentheses within the text. The essay appears in *Elizabeth Bishop: The Collected Prose*, edited, with an introduction, Robert Giroux (New York: Farrar, Straus, Giroux, 1984), 121–156.

2. Of this title, Lorrie Goldensohn in *Elizabeth Bishop: The Biography of a Poetry* (New York: Columbia University Press, 1992) remarks, "It is that yearning which is signally present even in Bishop's title of her account of the friendship in 'Efforts of Affection.' Her choice of a memoir essay, shows, among other things, one more indication of the limits of candor for her as a literary tool: the memoir will not provide a place for a total assessment either of the differences between their work or of Moore's impact on her own. But her essaying of affection will construct itself from feelings mixed in conflict and connection, or so the punning title for her memoir might tell us, borrowing as it does from a Moore poem identically named" (143).

3. Elizabeth Bishop in a letter to Robert Lowell, March 30, 1959 (The Houghton Library, Harvard University).

4. Melanie Klein, "Envy and Gratitude," *Envy and Gratitude and Other Works: 1946–1963* (London: The Hogarth Press and The Institute of Psycho-Analysis, 1975), 176–235.

5. See, for example, Bishop's "Songs for a Colored Singer, III," where an "Adult and child/sink to their rest./At sea the big ship sinks and dies,/lead in its breast" (49). And, in the second stanza where "the shadow of the crib makes an enormous cage/upon the wall." "At the Fishhouses" (64–66) ends with an image of the self drawing knowledge "from the cold hard mouth of the world, derived from the rocky breasts/forever, flowing and drawn, and since our knowledge is his-

torical, flowing, and flown." That knowledge should be drawn from the cold hard mouth, that it should be derived from rocky breasts, bespeaks a rigidity certainly antithetical to the nurturant reciprocal mutuality Klein associates with the ideal maternal relationship. Other instances of maternal displacement or negativity, the association of the maternal with aggression, can be found in "The Prodigal": "even to the sow that always ate her young—/till, sickening, he leaned to scratch her head," the mother's voice in "Squatter's Children," described as "ugly as sin—," and more pathetically in "Pink Dog," wherein the dog, in danger of losing her life and rendered an outcast "(a nursing mother, by those hanging teats)" is advised to seek disguise. Recall as well the description of breasts from "In the Waiting Room": "Their breasts were horrifying" (159). Note the moment from "Crusoe in England," when Crusoe experiments: "One day I dyed a baby goat bright red, with my red berries, just to see / something a little different. / And then his mother wouldn't recognize him" (165).

6. Goldensohn comments on Bishop's perception of Marianne Moore's relation to her mother, "Bishop was notably struck by the close sympathy emanating from Marianne's relationship with the elder Mrs. Moore. That closeness must frequently have intensified her own sense of isolation, especially as she realized that Moore's ethical code could never have embraced Bishop's own sexual choices, and stirred up old feelings of abandonment, as well as longing" (144).

7. For a more extensive discussion of "Invitation to Miss Marianne Moore," see the following chapter.

8. William Carlos Williams gave this description of Marianne Moore's appearance: "Marianne a stick of a woman, fence rail with a magnificent head of red hair (to the ground I imagine) fine eyes. Once bemoaned that God had given her no body at all to work with. Nothing feminine about her but the nervous movements, the brain, the eyes, the searching speech. A great personality lost because of devotion to—what the hell. Straight as an arrow in every way—wanting to be able to flex." Paul Mariani, *William Carlos Williams: A New World Naked* (New York: McGraw-Hill, 1981), 394. He would later refer to her as "the modern Andromeda—with her graying red hair all coiled about her brows," Mariani (395).

9. Elizabeth Bishop, *The Complete Poems: 1937–1979* (New York: Farrar, Straus, Giroux, 1983), 187.

10. Marianne Moore, *The Complete Poems* (New York: Macmillan, 1981), 121.

11. See "Efforts of Affection," 136.

12. Bishop, *The Complete Poems*, "Questions of Travel," 93–94.

13. Goldensohn notes Bishop's editing Hopkins' letter to Robert Bridges, ". . . so that in her extract Hopkins opens with his remarks about the "ungentlemanliness of poets and men of art," and excises "Hopkins' explicit Christianity" (151).

14. Invoking a letter from Gerard Manley Hopkins to Robert Bridges on the ideal of the "gentleman" (note the transposition of gender as Bishop appropriates the already old-fashioned term "gentleman" for the equally arcane "lady"), Bishop alludes to the highly suggestive relationship between the reticent Jesuit priest and his adversarial friend, a relationship that extended over time and involved a detailed often painful scrutiny of each other's work—a relationship forged by dependency and aggression. Responding to Bridge's harsh questioning of "The Wreck of the *Deutschland*," the poem that broke his extended self-imposed silence, Hopkins nevertheless insists that Bridges remains his sole audience: "I cannot think of altering anything. Why shd. I? I do not write for the public. You are my public and I hope to convert you" (144; see letter to Robert Bridges, August 21, 1877). The friendship between the reclusive Hopkins and the poet-laureate-to-be cannot help but suggest parallels with the Moore/Bishop relationship: mutual scrutiny of the work, Moore's/Hopkins' selective disengagement from public as well as from heterosexual life—both are pertinent to Bishop's friendship with Moore. The passage Bishop introduces on the ideal of the "gentleman" or the "artist versus the gentleman" question, moreover, reintroduces the issues that have remained unresolved throughout the memoir: how to determine an ethical standard by which one is to live a life devoted to art, a subject, as I have already noted, in which Moore has offered rather problematic instruction.

15. Of the conclusion to Bishop's essay, Goldensohn remarks, "The figure in the world that one cuts *matters*. Artists are not different from other people; whereof one cannot speak, perhaps it is best to remain silent. And yet what is the eventual price paid by the poet when so much of her life lies under heavy guard? The guardedness could be viewed as a tragic evisceration of subject, not entirely a result of free choice made by the poet, but of choices imposed by the manners and morals and muddles of the people among whom one lives and publishes. Finally, if one cannot trust one's own chosen mentor-mother, it must be a very carefully drawn circle that *can* be trusted" (151–152).

16. Klein is absolutely clear on the temporal and psychic primacy of the mother-child relationship for determining the later Oedipal stage; the mother remains the formative figure in the originatory psychological paradigm. When writing of the Oedipal phase, Klein notes that "among the features of the earliest stage of the Oedipus complex are the phantasies of the mother's breast and the mother containing the

penis of the father, or the father containing the mother. This is the basis of the combined parent figure," *Envy and Gratitude*, 197.

17. Goldensohn (144) cites Bonnie Costello's emphasis on "the centrally female verb 'nurture' as the word that characterizes Moore's relationship to Bishop" (see Bonnie Costello, "Marianne Moore and Elizabeth Bishop: Friendship and Influence," in Harold Bloom, ed., *Marianne Moore* [New York: Chelsea House, 1987], 120). My discussion engages the dynamics of nurturance to emphasize its ambivalent and conflictual aspects.

CHAPTER TWO

1. David Kalstone in his sensitive and illuminating study, *Becoming a Poet: Elizabeth Bishop with Marianne Moore and Robert Lowell* (New York: Farrar, Straus, Giroux, 1989), notes Bishop's "interiorizing" interest in her notebook entries of 1934 and 1935, as well as her early poems' "psychological and subjective cast" (12).

2. All letters cited in this chapter are from Bishop's unpublished letters to Robert Lowell, The Lowell Collection, Houghton Library, Harvard University.

3. See Bishop's copy at the Houghton Library, Harvard University.

4. See Bishop's copy of Moore's volume at the Houghton Library.

5. This postcard is in the possession of Sandra McPherson, The University of California, Davis.

6. See Bishop's copy of this volume at the Houghton Library.

7. Kalstone mentions a number of affinities between Moore's and Bishop's work. See, for example, his reading of Moore's "The Paper Nautilus" and Bishop's "Jeronimo's House" (70–72 and 86–101 *passim*).

8. Of this last stanza, Bonnie Costello observes, "The impersonal, phallic but impotent 'Man,' the inverted pin, is displaced by the still distanced but more personal 'you,' a generalization offered to the reader of the speaker's own experience. The inverted pin is turned over to the Man-Moth, in whose possession it becomes a potent, vaguely phallic but also feminine tear, 'like the bee's sting,' painful to the receiver, perhaps fatal to the bestower, yet 'cool as from underground springs and pure enough to drink.' The beholder is now the questing hero, drinking the redemptive waters of expressed feeling" (54). A gift that is painful to the recipient recalls the terms operating in the psychodynamics of Kleinian reciprocity wherein the child fears that the gift she bestows upon the mother has the potential to do her irreparable harm. The phallic associations of the inverted pin converted into the tear suggest the combined forces of penetration and

absorption as well as the conflictual ambivalence that governs the dynamics of gift-giving.

9. See the preceding chapter's discussion of "Envy and Gratitude."

10. For an extended discussion, see the following chapter.

11. Moore, not surprisingly, diverges in registering this difference, remarking to Bishop, "I do feel that tentativeness and interiorizing are your dangers as well as your strength" (see Kalstone, 59).

12. Drawing a distinction between the cloud and the gull on the one hand and the unbeliever, on the other, Robert Dale Parker suggests that "By not believing, he [the unbeliever] implicitly chooses his precarious masthead of imaginative risk; at least he chooses it over the cloud's and the gull's certainty." See Robert Dale Parker, *The Unbeliever: The Poetry of Elizabeth Bishop* (Urbana and Chicago: University of Illinois Press, 1988), 33.

13. Concluding her discussion of "Invitation to Miss Marianne Moore," Bonnie Costello notes, "Bishop is not Marianne Moore, the daytime comet above the world, reimagining it in terms of moral and aesthetic ideals. Her glance is always within the world, partial, troubled, inquiring. Repeatedly her eye confronts a terrifying darkness, an 'entire night' along its path, but turns from it, toward life and movement" (45).

Chapter Three

1. For a comprehensive treatment of the subjects discussed in this chapter see Christopher Bollas, *The Shadow of the Object: Psychoanalysis of the Unthought Known* (New York: Columbia University Press, 1987). All page references refer to this volume.

2. See Melanie Klein, "Infantile Anxiety Situations Reflected in a Work of Art and in the Creative Impulse," *The Selected Melanie Klein*, ed. Juliet Mitchell (New York: The Free Press, 1987) 84–94. All future references to Klein's essay will occur in parentheses within the text.

3. Elizabeth Bishop, "In the Village," *The Collected Prose*, ed. Robert Giroux (New York: Farrar, Straus, Giroux, 1984), p. 237. All future references to "In the Village" will occur in parentheses within the text.

4. Of this scream, Thomas Travisano notes, "The scream seems to fade, to be 'almost lost.' But among all those correlatives for pain that it recalls, 'things damaged and lost, sickened or destroyed,' this story's very existence shows that the 'frail almost-lost scream' still vibrates in memory as it lives in the sky." See Thomas J. Travisano, *Elizabeth Bishop: Her Artistic Development* (Charlottesville: University Press of Virginia, 1988), 172.

5. Klein, "Mourning and Its Relation to Manic-Depressive States," *Selected Klein*, 156.

6. Ibid., 162.

7. Ibid.

Conclusion

1. For an overview of this branch of psychoanalysis, see Jay R. Greenberg and Stephen A. Mitchell, *Object Relations in Psychoanalytic Theory* (Cambridge: Harvard University Press, 1983). Of the various theorists, I have found Melanie Klein and Christopher Bollas (whose work is not included in Greenberg and Mitchell) to be the most pertinent to literary studies.